DO THE TEN COMMANDMENTS HAVE A UNIVERSAL SIGNIFICANCE?

God's Law as the Basis of a Global Culture

DO THE TEN COMMANDMENTS HAVE A UNIVERSAL SIGNIFICANCE?

God's Law as the Basis of a Global Culture

Daniel V. Porter

With a Foreword by
Samuel H. Larsen

The Edwin Mellen Press
Lewiston•Queenston•Lampeter

Library of Congress Cataloging-in-Publication Data

Porter, Daniel V.
    Do the Ten commandments have a universal significance? : God's law as the basis of a
global culture / Daniel V. Porter ; with a foreword by Samuel H. Larsen.
        p. cm.
    Includes bibliographical references (p.   ) and index.
    ISBN-13: 978-0-7734-1389-4 (alk. paper)
    ISBN-10: 0-7734-1389-8 (alk. paper)
    1. Ten commandments. I. Title.
    BV4655.P63 2011
    241.5'2--dc22

                            2010054269

hors série.

A CIP catalog record for this book is available from the British Library.

The Edwin Mellen Press   The Edwin Mellen Press
          Box 450   Box 67
    Lewiston, New York   Queenston, Ontario
     USA 14092-0450   CANADA L0S 1L0

                    The Edwin Mellen Press, Ltd.
                    Lampeter, Ceredigion, Wales
                    UNITED KINGDOM SA48 8LT

                 Printed in the United States of America

DEDICATION

I dedicate this study to my wife of 43 years. She is God's grace to me.

TABLE OF CONTENTS

LIST OF FIGURES

Figure

LIST OF TABLES

Tables

FOREWORD

D.V. Porter's research is an original line of inquiry. He has addressed a fundamental question: Is the Decalogue a cross-cultural moral transcendent, or is it culture-specific and historically confined? To put it differently, are the Ten Commandments culturally relative, or are they morally absolute across cultures and historical periods? Do they have anything to tell us about our own–and other–cultures?

Interestingly, the Ten Commandments as given in Exodus chapter twenty do not deal with the specifics of sabbath worship, but only the creationally grounded sabbath principle (later reaffirmed in Deuteronomy and connected as well to the context of Israel's deliverance). The majority of Christians have historically understood the Ten Commandments to be universal in intent and applicability.

Neither do the Ten Commandments contain any reference to tabernacle or temple worship, or to sacrifice, or to purification rites (including circumcision, which was instituted long before Moses in the time of Abraham, or ceremonial washings). Those regulations may be viewed as a Mosaic cultural application and expression of the Ten Commandments for Israel as that nation journeyed through its trajectory in redemptive history. The Ten Commandments themselves comprise, arguably, the universal moral and ethical umbrella beneath which the Mosaic laws in their particulars are contextually subsumed. The Westminster Shorter Catechism states: "The moral law is summarily comprehended in the Ten Commandments" (WSC #41).

The NT teaches that the Mosaic laws in their particulars are fulfilled and superseded in Christ, yet nowhere treats the moral universality of the Ten Commandments as having been abrogated. The particularistic Mosaic laws are said to be fulfilled–and superseded–in Christ. The Ten Commandments, on the other hand, are presented as satisfied only by Christ (and in Christ, who is himself "the LORD our righteousness"), without removing the divine standard for moral purity and justice that reflect the character of a holy God ("you shall be holy, because I the LORD your God am holy").

Indeed, the Ten Commandments can only be rightly understood and obeyed in the context of humanity's relationship with the Creator, that is to say, covenantally. Hence, the Ten Commandments, argues Porter, constitute a universal cross-cultural diagnostic, a moral and ethical "litmus test," as it were, of culture and worldview. That is to say, the Ten Commandments are a divinely given cultural ethnohermeneutic that both corrects and teaches life in covenant with the Creator.

Dr. Porter has designed a diagnostic instrument based upon the Ten Commandments as a covenantal ethnohermeneutic and has applied it across three cultures (case studies) set in vastly different historical periods: OT Israel, NT Gentiles, and modern urbanites. He has then applied literary analysis of the OT and NT documents, comparing the results with a similar analysis of documents transcribed from ethnographic interviews and focus groups of modern urban residents of Atlanta, Georgia.

Porter's conclusions are significant. In his own words, "Twenty-first century urbanites voice worldview assumptions and opinions startlingly similar to descriptions of Israelites by Moses and of Gentiles by Paul. The replicative test results argue for the validity of the biblical Covenant to provide reliable guidance in an environment of competing worldviews."

In an age in which it is fashionable to deny any transcendent moral and ethical absolutes or any standard by which to measure cultures and societies, Porter offers us a fresh perspective on why, and how, the Ten Commandments are timeless and relevant to all cultures in all ages. I highly commend his work as well worth reading.

Samuel H. Larsen, D.Min., Ph.D.
Samuel Patterson Professor of Missions and Evangelism
Reformed Theological Seminary, Jackson, Mississippi

PREFACE

Do the Ten Commandments Have a Universal Significance?
God's Law as the Basis of a Global Culture
D. V. Porter

This is a research project set within the conversation regarding where to locate Christianity. The project employs integrative research methodology, chiefly textual analysis and qualitative interviewing to study the potential of one of the most ancient of biblical givens, the Ten Commandments, to accurately differentiate worldviews in the twenty-first century. In order to explore a comprehensive theory of ethnohermeneutics and to test the reliability of the instrument, the researcher replicates similar analysis across three case studies of three different cultural scenes in three periods of history. The results are clear, if preliminary. Twenty-first century urbanites voice worldview assumptions and opinions startlingly similar to descriptions of Israelites by Moses and of Gentiles by Paul. The replicative test results argue for the validity of the biblical Covenant to provide reliable guidance in an environment of competing worldviews.

ACKNOWLEDGEMENTS

Umberto Cassuto, Lloyd Davies, my chair Sam Larsen, Franco Maggiotto, David Naugle, Robert Nisbet, Anders Nygren, and Joel Rosenberg, in particular, provided insightful directions for this study. I could not have done this study without the support of my life-long partner and friend, my wife, Bonnie. Her editorial skills and insightful mind were invaluable in the actual writing.

1

CHAPTER 1

INTRODUCTION

Background and Significance of the Research

Globalization and diversity emerged in the late twentieth century to dominate the scene in the early part of the new century. Due to its apparent lack of consistency, however, the combination phenomenon has not met the challenge of spiraling catastrophes, contextualisms, and chaos throughout the world. Nor has it been kind to Christianity, guilty by association with Modernism. Driven by their common worldview, globalization and diversity have taken their toll on the world's oldest and perhaps largest human association, the Church. It seems to be surviving, if barely, its total numbers having just edged out overall population growth. However, the Church has accomplished this mainly by extending its reach in non-Western parts of the world. The Western Church cannot continue hemorrhaging large numbers of its population to autonomy, independent spirituality and atheism, and expect to fulfill its God-given mandate to make disciples of all nations.

Research Concern

With the passing of the old Christian consensus, most Western Christians have adapted to globalization and diversity by simultaneously conducting their lives on two distinct and unreconciled levels. On one level, they are members of a church and subscribe to a statement of faith. Below their system of conscious beliefs, however, lies a deeper level of embedded traditions and customs derived from their upbringing in their native culture.[1]

---

[1] Paul Hiebert first studied this phenomenon among "young" churches planted by Westerners. The concept was first used by Father Jaime Bulato (1962) and later elaborated on the concept in his 1992 book *Split-Level Christianity*. Cf., also Stackhouse 1988, 114.

This dualism occurs in large part because of a fundamental misunderstanding about reality popularized by Enlightenment thinking [2] and compounded by the Church's failure to adapt its hermeneutic accordingly in a biblically appropriate manner. [3] The common *mis*perception of reality is twofold: (1) one's native cultural worldview is the way things *are* in this world, or close to it (Hiebert et al. 1999, 27; cf., Barrs 1982, 3-12); and (2) the Bible is often viewed merely as a collection of *ideas* (Stackhouse 1988, 3), consigned to the speculative realm of opinion (Modern), or to personal choice (Postmodern).

The Church failed to sufficiently address the Enlightenment and subsequent erosion of all that Luther and Calvin had recovered. Instead, it responded by redoubling its efforts based on a hermeneutic geared to older reformational times, primarily concerned with clarifying the relationship between true faith and the "christianist" belief and lifestyle that generations had internalized during the Middle Ages and had come to accept as normal Christian living. [4]

Unanswered epistemological problems, such as autonomy based on reason and the Kantian split, opened the door. Increasingly, a new version of believism,

---

2 The Greek, and subsequently Enlightenment, thinkers, "valued the life of *theoria* above *poesis* and *praxis* as that form of knowing that was most like the life of God." Plato's and Aristotle's "preference for *theoria* induced a disjunction between the three" (Stackhouse 1988, 88). In the Enlightenment it forced a dualism of either Reason (Descartes) or Empiricism (Locke), and later between Idealism (Kant) or Materialism (Marx). Jane Cary Peck notes another example of the dualism: "Posing the question [of community or individual] in this 'either/or' way, as many do today, is more a reflection of the Enlightenment division of *psyche* from *polis* than the biblical view of person in community" (Ibid., 80).

3 The Church's response since the Reformation has tended to follow one of several lines of thought: (1) theology is understood to have no knowable referent (Nominalism); (2) a "scientific" theology with facts and provable absolutes (Positivism); (3) a metaphysical-moral realm transcendent to and possibly immanent in the empirical world (Kantian Dualism); more recently (4) theology is derived *from* local contexts, not brought *into (Sitz im leben);* (5) redemptive *praxis* is kernel or source of theological inquiry (Liberation) (Stackhouse 1988).

4 Hermeneutics was supposed to support, secure, and clarify an already accepted understanding (Kimmerle 1967). Additionally, hermeneutics was primarily prophetic, geared to reforming the Church and reviving the soul (see Packer 1990; Ryken 1986; e.g., *The Larger Catechism,* Question 97).

without consequent worldview and lifestyle change, has reasserted itself once again. Christians dispersed throughout the world's human cultures cannot live on two unreconcilable levels if they are to live as God's covenant people and disciple those around them. Puritanism no longer is the norm by which the broader culture, worldview, can be evaluated. The biblical covenant must be revisited with fresh minds.

This study compares worldview theory and its current usage with the Covenant and consequent covenantal way of life described in Scripture. It explores how the Ten Words (Instructions) are used to induct new believers into the covenant community and covenantal way of life. At the same time, it explores how the Ten Words indirectly critique their home culture worldviews.

Research Question

The Research Question of this study is: What is the role of the Ten Commandments in discipling the nations? Five subsidiary questions are asked of three cultural scenes or case studies: (1) What/who is the focus of the case study? (2) What does the transcript itself report of the participants' former way of life (worldview), and what covenantal instruction from the Ten Words is needed? (3) What does the Covenant entail, of what does the covenantal way of life consist, and how is this new way different from their old way of life? (4) By what means are the Ten Words used to instruct the participants? (5) To what extent are the Covenant or the Ten Words used to instruct the participants and in what ways are they instruments of grace?

Definitions of Key Terms

Culture. Catch-all word, defined various ways in anthropological and sociological literature: by artifacts, by social systems, by communication and meaning, and so on. For the purposes of this study, culture will be understood to represent the collective output and shared meaning of a community living and

4

working together over time. While every social unit, to some extent, has its own culture, for this study culture will be taken as reflecting a community, a larger people group, or a nation. Although each "culture" is considered unique in at least some ways, not the least by its members, a culture is not static but somewhat fluid or porous.

Worldview. Two usages: (1) The popular sense, an idea or picture of how reality is perceived by the current culture to help its members live successfully in their world. (2) The modern technical discussion of worldview, which generally includes (a) universal mental categories; (b) reality visually and symbolically grasped; (c) understood to be tacit; (d) used to predict behavior or vice versa, and therefore can be usable in worldview transformation. Most Christian and other theorists assume that the term is neutral (i.e., can be used by Christian perspective or by any other), and so attempt to imbue it with Christian meaning and application. This study utilizes "worldview" in that technical sense for communication purposes.

Given. Known fact (in the older realist sense, e.g., Stackhouse 1988, 24), such as a historic event like the covenant bond established between God and Abraham; an object such as a book or monument; something bestowed or conferred; or the archaic usage: an enactment into law. Some biblical givens, understood to be bounded on either side by eternity: Creation; original sin and expulsion from the Garden; the Flood; the Abrahamic Covenant; the Passover and the Exodus from Egypt, and the Ten Words; the birth, crucifixion, resurrection and ascension of Jesus Christ; the promise of the Spirit given at Pentecost; Scripture itself; the Last Judgment, including the fiery cleansing of creation.

Givens are pre-critical and structural, that is, coming before or into human conventions, social structures, and relations. In this study, givens are contrasted generally with the assumptions or assertions of worldview theory. Through our upbringing, these assumptions come to us from the mist of ancient history. They are a mixture of truth, half-truth, and error: facts based on experience and scientific observation, the wisdom of the elders, folk tales, origin stories, old wives' tales, customs, laws, and so forth that combine to make up the cultural story or wisdom of a people or culture. Ultimately, worldview wisdom is unprovable, and, in many cases, unfalsifiable, but is assumed or asserted to be the way things really are. The Covenant, in particular, functions for members of the covenant community similarly to the way worldview functions for others.

Monism. Used in this study in the general background sense; a basic worldview assumption: there is only one reality, all reality is one, singular, including even a god concept; everything is inherent within a closed system, with no "other." Monism is inimical to every non-monistic understanding, including a covenantal, or biblical and trinitarian, monotheistic understanding. Monists perpetuate their assumption in two ways: (1) completely eradicate and replace one way with another; or (2) merge one way with another and over time synthesize them into one. Van Til points out the differences between biblical and non-theist (monist) understanding of such terminologies and processes as "synthesis," "integration," "accommodation," and "inductive" and "deductive" reasoning. Furthermore, his argument is that any reasoning whatsoever that does not begin with theistic presuppositions will ultimately devolve into monistic thinking (Van Til 1954, 1955). Other terms in this study such as "subsume," "conflate," "choice," and "complementarity" are likewise co-opted to their agenda.

Law/Commandment. Words and usage in the Old and New Testaments indicate that the Law or Commandments are intended to be something like 'instructional stipulations' (of a mutual commitment, see Kline). The creative core of God's Covenant, the Law was originally referred to as the ten "Words" of God, spoken and written from Mt. Sinai to the children of Israel after their deliverance from Egypt, around 1400 B.C. Expanded to include 613 case laws and the history of Israel's origins, the Ten Words formed the core of what became known as the Mosaic Instructions, or Torah.[5] The Law was thus instructional in nature but

---

5 Torah: (תּוֹרָה) "instruction;" used of the five books of Moses.

carried the weight of divine orders. By Jesus' day the Law was used also as a synecdoche for all of Scripture, for the whole counsel of God. During the Inter-testamental period the Torah, Law, had also become distorted as the criteria, if not the mediator, of righteousness before God.

Both Jesus and Paul teach against confusing righteousness with obeying God's instructional stipulations to gain merit before God in order to gain eternal life. Instead, they emphasize the given nature of the Law and necessity of following it. Paul also teaches that God uses the Law to bring a person to the point of learning human perfidy and God's provision of grace "in Christ" alone (Gal 4).[6]

Covenant. Mendenhall (1954), Kline (1968), and Weinfeld (1973) have elaborated covenantal parallels with Hittite treaties, but these have received scant notice thus far in the academic community. According to the biblical account, covenant was first explicitly established by God with Abraham (Gn 12, 15), although may have been present in the origin of creation. For this study, covenant is God's presence in the midst of his people; it is God's purpose for humankind. Covenant is loyal commitment, a relationship with God. Covenant, along with covenantal way of life, will be elaborated further in the literature review.

Covenantal way of life. Places priority on living in relation to God and his ways, the One who comes to humankind and promises to be with his people forever. Within the world of human cultures, God is establishing the beginnings of a new culture of a completely different kind, the precursor of his future actual reign on the "new" earth (Dt 32:47).

---

6 Due to delimitations, a review of the literature on the Ten Commandments *per se*, or of the biblical understanding of the Law is not provided. Nonetheless, these principal works were consulted: *The Ten Commandments in recent research* (Stamm 1967); *The Ten Commandments for Today* (Barclay 1973); *John Calvin's Sermons on the Ten Commandments* (Farley 1980); *The Christian Way of Living: An Ethics of the Ten Commandments* (Bockmuehl 1994); *The Ten Commandments in History: Mosaic Paradigms for a Well-Ordered Society* (Kuntz 2004); *I Am the Lord Your God: Christian Reflections on the Ten Commandments* (Braaten and Seitz 2005); as well as the reference works: ABD, BGAD, TDOT, NIDOTTE.

Hermeneutic. Theory or method of interpretation, usually of texts, also of cultures; from Greek (*hermeneutikos*, *hermeneuein* "interpret"). The theory one brings to the text, to interpret the text in light of the context, or to interpret the text to the context. Hermeneutics is more context, or present environment-oriented, than exegesis. It can be argued that every interpreter has a viewpoint, which is assumed in this study.

Ethnohermeneutics. How differences in context, environment, worldview assumptions, affect understanding of the text or of other horizons. It is the interpreter becoming aware of her own glasses. The goal: that the audience, from their particular worldview assumptions, approximate an understanding of the original intent of the author for the original audience.

Covenantal ethnohermeneutics. A more appropriately biblical approach to understanding the triadic relationship between Scripture, the covenant community of believers, and the unevangelized peoples of the world (Edmondson 2005); analyzes other worldviews and cultures in relation to the biblical covenant.

Believer/member of the covenant community. The entirety of biblical and human history is spanned by the Covenant. All believers are together in covenant. Jesus and the apostles stood in covenant with Old Testament believers, and we stand in covenant with both (Davies 1997, 387). The New Covenant in Jesus' blood and resurrection inaugurated a new order of life for all peoples. From among any people, all who respond to his call are made members of the covenant community (1 Cor 12:12-13; Eph 3:12-22; Gal 3:26-29).

Discipling the nations. Jesus Christ commanded his followers, beginning with the apostles: "As you go, make disciples of all peoples, baptizing them in the name of the Father and of the Son and of the Holy Spirit, teaching them to obey everything I commanded you. And surely I am with you always, to the very end of the age" (Mt 28:19-20); this can be said to summarize the ministry of the Church.

Assumptions

The fundamental assumption of this study is the otherness of God. That is, God was prior to and outside of, different from, whatever he subsequently made. This affects everything else we can know (other scholars with similar assumptions: Collison 1985; Kaiser 1987, 6). For example, humankind and all created reality are not the same as, or part of God, nor do they include God. We cannot approach God; rather, he comes to us.

The researcher assumes that the prior issue for research is the relationship of the finite, knowing subject with God, the Creator. The secondary issue of research is the relationship of the finite knowing subject and the finite object to be known (Van Til 1954, 14). Profitable research is that which has realistic but significant aims, corresponds to or answers essential research questions, is undergirded by the most relevant and reliable theory available, and is conducted according to rigorous care and standards.

This researcher also assumes that definitions and research methodology do not establish truth, whether concerning God or anything else. Rather, by these the researcher tries to faithfully explicate what truth, or parts of truth, can be known (cf. Stackhouse 1988, 154, 174). Data, therefore, must not be interpreted in such a way that it (a) claims to trump or control what God is doing; or (b) implies that it is all that God is doing.

There is a paucity of explicit references in the literature linking biblical understanding to scientific method, such as case study. Nevertheless, this silence should not be taken to signify that no such link exists. This study assumes biblical guidance and warrant for any inquiry and attempts to strengthen the link between the two.

Limitations and Delimitations

This study is limited to the existing literature on the theories of ethnohermeneutics, biblical covenant, and worldview, and to the case studies of three populations, two in the biblical literature and one in contemporary America. Out of all the possibilities of study within these fields and cases, and of the possible self-disclosure of the respondents, the findings are delimited to a comparison of worldview and covenant, and the implications for what can be termed covenantal ethnohermeneutics. The literature on Federal Theology, the Ten Commandments as Law, and so forth, will not be covered, as an example. In a further effort to limit the scope, this study delimits the dynamics of transformation from its inquiry into the what and to what extent believers may be inducted into the covenantal way of life.

The research findings are not generalizable to populations beyond the three populations or cultural scenes defined in the research design or to areas of study outside the parameters of the research. However, they may be generalizable to worldview, covenant, and hermeneutic theory.

CHAPTER 2

REVIEW OF THE LITERATURE

Three horizons are triangulated in the review of literature (figure 1) in order to multiply perspectives, approximate reliability and validity, and strengthen theory. The Bible is considered the main reference point or locus of meaning and

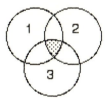

Figure 1. Three literature horizons

final court of appeal (Van Til 1955, 35). The Bible is also the primary literature source for biblical ontology, particularly with regard to the Covenant and the covenantal way of life and for the two case studies reflecting the horizon of Moses and Paul.[7]

In order to study two related contemporary American cultural scenes, secondary literature of biblical ontology is consulted as well: contemporary ethnohermeneutics and worldview theory; and integrative and qualitative social science theory, particularly case study.

---

[7] It is recognized that thinkers such as Rogers and Caldwell take the existence of multiple worldviews or variations of worldview in the Bible to mean that one worldview is not taught. This will be addressed in the research findings.

Purpose and Design of the Literature Review

The chief task, ultimately, of reviewing germane precedent literature in a scholarly study is to develop or strengthen theory. It can accomplish this by integrating the most significant available literature and by providing a conceptual framework to more fully understand the research question and methodology. A further function of literature review is to assess whether previous theory can and does contribute to resolving the research question(s) and, if so, to what extent. Finally, the literature can document the relevance and validity (i.e., warrant) of the research question.

For these reasons, this review is conducted primarily by interweaving the various works into a thematic outline, rather than the approach of summarizing and assessing each principal author or work separately. This particularly lends itself to the subject of the biblical covenant.

Biblical Ontology

The first horizon or area of literature to be reviewed is biblical ontology. Classic covenant theorists include Calvin, Turretin (1679-85), the Puritans such as John Owen (1668, 1684), the Princetonians such as Hodge (1871-1873), and the Continental theologians such as Bavinck (1895) and Kuyper (1899). They posit that Scripture teaches one perpetual covenant between God and man, successively renewed, covering all peoples of the world, extending to all generations of human history (not one covenant of grace as interpreted by Barth and Murray). The Covenant and consequent way of life is not just a good idea or something well reasoned out. A survey of the literature, biblical and secondary, suggests that it is instead grounded on the pillars, or givens, of Scripture: key persons, episodes of God's redemptive activity, institutions, and texts. This study will concentrate on the very beginnings of Reformed theology (Calvin) and on its most recent interlocutors who are rediscovering links with older Jewish understandings of covenant.

The Covenant between God and Man

Beginning with Abraham, God established a perpetual covenant with his chosen people. The following three paragraphs describe the basic characteristics of the Covenant.

The essence of the Covenant is the presence of the Lord among his people (Jer 7) (Leuchter 2005, 98). God is in covenant loyalty-love (*hesed*) relationship with his chosen people. This Christian understanding is traced as far back as the seventeenth century in the writings of John Cocceius (Robertson 1980, 5). In the *Institutes*, Calvin identifies what he calls the "very formula of the Covenant": "I will be your God and you shall be my people" (Lv 26:12) (Calvin 1960, II.10.8). The Covenant is constituted (Robertson: "formalized") with an oath, signifying the inviolable bond (cf. Ps 89:3, 34f; 105:8-10) (Robertson 1980, 6-7) with which he binds himself to his chosen people.

The Covenant reveals God's purpose for humankind. In other words, it expresses that God's purpose is covenantal (Eph 1). Furthermore, "this single covenant is, for Calvin, always and everywhere a covenant of grace" (Edmondson 2005, 6). Covenant, or covenantal, came to signify "promise-fulfillment" (cf. Muller 1990, 81, n. 41).[8]

These, then, are the predominant descriptors of the Covenant in the literature: the very presence of God among all covenant peoples, characterized by a hesed relationship. He is our God and we are his people, bound together by an inviolable oath. His covenantal purpose is always and everywhere grace and the fulfillment of his promises.

Mediation of the Covenant

"Apart from the Mediator, God never showed favor toward the ancient people, nor ever gave hope of grace to them" (Calvin 1960, II.VI.2). Christ, as the Mediator of the Covenant, authored it, carried it in his own body on the cross,

---

8 Some note two; cf. *The Westminster Confession of Faith*, 3d ed.

and is the end at which it is aimed (Gn 12:3) (Edmondson 2005, 6). Christ's mediatorship appears to be necessary to bridge the ontological and sin gaps between God and humankind. Only one who is truly God and truly man could bring the two together. The Covenant is the seal of this reconciliation. Now we know that covenant relationship is only possible in Christ through the Holy Spirit. Furthermore, Christ's declaration on the Cross, "It is finished!" effected the oath of the Covenant. Because of the inviolable bond of his own character and Word (Heb 6), the covenant relationship between God and humans is reality.

The Covenant was successively renewed several times in Scripture and spans the entirety of human redemption. Reflecting God himself, the Covenant itself is one, singular, and perpetual. "Calvin never describes [the covenants] as new or separate covenants; rather, they were renewals of the one eternal covenant that God made with Abraham in Abraham's original call" (Edmondson 2005, 24). Robertson adds: "No period in the history of redemption from Noah to Christ stands outside the realm of God's covenantal dealings with his people" (1980, 17).

The successive covenant renewals made with Abraham, Moses, David, and the Messiah span the entirety of biblical and human redemptive history. Edmondson explains:

> In the covenant, God gave God's people a land, a law, and a king,
> and through these gifts and promises God called the Church to
> look for a greater enactment and manifestation of God's mercy that
> was to come in Christ. (Edmondson 2005, 5)

Scripture cites five to seven renewals, depending on the selector's criteria: (1) with Moses on Mt. Sinai (Ex 20ff); (2) with the next generation, first through Moses (Dt) and then through Joshua, before going into the land (Jos 5); (3) possibly, through Samuel with Israel marking the end of the Judges and transition to kingship (1 Sm 7); (4) with the "house of David" (2 Sm 7); (5) possibly with Josiah (2 Kgs 22; 2 Chr 34-35); (6) possibly with the returned exiles (Ezr 3 and 6; Neh 8-9); and (7) consummated in Christ (Mt 26:28; Mk 14:24; Lk 22:20). Each renewal maintains continuity with the one covenant, and reinforces it. Several, notably the Mosaic, Davidic and New covenants, further develop the Covenant, bringing new elements and expanding the meaning.

Edmondson poses the question: "How did God use biblical persons, institutions, events, and texts in relationship to and presentation of Christ to work out God's merciful purpose within the context of God's covenant relationship with the Church?" (Edmondson 2005, 15). This will be answered more fully in the literature on the covenantal way of life. However, it appears that these gifts and promises, and these persons, events, and institutions, including the law and the land, and the texts are the pillars or foundations, which this study refers to as givens, to serve God's chosen people as covenant signs and seals.

The New Covenant in Jesus' blood and resurrection inaugurated a new order of life, the covenantal way of life, and explicitly extended it for all peoples (Mt 28:18-20). First, the New Covenant fully addresses the "ultimate crisis of human existence" (Horton 2002, 181, n. 47): separation from God. Paul's letter to the Ephesians offers a typical example. Before, the Ephesians were foreigners to the Covenant, separate from Christ, but now they are brought near and included in Christ, as one of the new peoples to the Covenant (Eph 2:12-13) (Gräbe 2006, 215). Romans and Galatians in particular explore how the original covenant members, Israel, are related to the New Covenant members, formerly known by Jews as the Gentiles or "uncircumcision."[9] Second, both Christ himself and his work on the Cross fulfill centuries of promise. He invites all chosen peoples to enter and live in that promise.

In recent years, some Jewish and Christian scholars (e.g., Davies, Edmondson, and Leuchter) have begun to look afresh at Paul's statement that

---

9 This, too, was in God's plan from the beginning. It was foretold long beforehand in such pronouncements as "The earth is the Lord's and everything in it" (Ps 24:1). Jesus clarified other Old Testament prophecies (e.g., Is 11:10; 52:15; 56:7; 60-66; Hos 1:10; 2:23) when he declared the temple to be a house of prayer for all nations (Mt 21:13), and when, in his inaugural sermon at Nazareth, he left no doubt about including Gentiles (Lk 4:14-30) in the "kingdom of God."

"theirs is the adoption as sons; theirs the divine glory, the covenants, the receiving of the law, the temple worship and the promises" (Rom 9:4). They affirm Paul: *All* are now together in one covenant. As Davies expresses it, Jesus and the apostles stood in covenant with Old Testament prophets and writers, and we stand in covenant with both (1997, 387).

The Covenant Leads to an Entire Way of Life

The covenantal (kingdom) bond between God and man leads to an entire new way of life for all covenant peoples in every culture and generation. The Mosaic Covenant constitutes the covenantal charter. Moses wrote that observance of the Torah is a covenant of life (Dt 32:46-47) (Hoffecker 2008). It can be said that the Jewish way of life was constituted in the Mosaic Covenant (Currid 2007). The Ten Words were spoken and written by God from Mt. Sinai. Subsequently, they were expanded into hundreds of case laws that covered every aspect of life as it was then lived (Kaiser 1987, 164-65; Kreitzer 1996, 48). Over time, the Torah, the Covenant, became the actual mental categories of a covenantal way of life (Currid 2007, 68). As they did for Israel at the forging of the Mosaic Covenant almost two and a half millennia prior, the Ten Words serve as anchor points (Hoffecker 2008) for the covenantal way of life today.

The Covenant provides a framework for and way of living based on pillars or foundations, givens, which serve as signs and seals of covenant renewal and reminders. Scholars note that covenant renewals are inaugurated or accompanied by signs and seals intended to aid remembrance.[10] "The signs of the covenant [circumcision, Sabbath, kingship, baptism, the Lord's Supper] symbolize the permanence of the bond between God and his people" (Robertson 1980, 7), as well as hint at the nature of those renewals. Edmondson concurs:

---

10 Stackhouse notes that symbols are "multileveled" and cannot easily be reduced. This is not to agree, as he also says, that they are the primary language of theology (Stackhouse 1988).

The prescription of circumcision to Abraham, the Law given to
Moses, and the eternal kingship promised to David were bound to
God's original covenant and were intended to recall it to the minds
of the people, that it might be etched there with certainty.
(Edmondson 2005, 6)

National pillars, givens, such as the Ten Words, Judges, Prophets, Kings,
Priests, Temple and Jerusalem, undergird covenant continuity and way of life.
Many of the prophetical sermons were in covenantal terms: fidelity to *YHWH*,
communal responsibility, social justice, and so forth (Leuchter 2005, 99). For
example, Jeremiah, a nobleman and prophet at the very end of the monarchy, ca.
600 B.C., expressed covenantal understanding in his so-called Temple Sermon
(Leuchter 2005, 94; see Hos 4:9; 12:3ff). While Babylon waited outside to storm
the gates, he repeats the entire Ten in that sermon, calling Judah's leaders one last
time to repentance.

The cycle of daily sacrifices, family teaching, weekly Sabbath, and feast
days throughout the year also served as covenant reminders, or renewals. One of
the best known and loved is the Passover meal, the annual remembrance of God's
protective act of "passing over" Israel on the provisional basis of the blood of a
"cut" lamb. Now known by Christians as the Lord's Supper, we remember Jesus
propitiating God on the basis of his own blood on the cross (Robertson 1980, 13).
All of these observances combined to create an environment, a daily, weekly, and
yearly rhythm that undergirded the *Sh'ma* instructions, and contributed to building
a memory cache of covenant, a way of thinking and living, analogous to
worldview.

There is ample evidence in Jewish literature that Torah observance
became, for late Judaism (Second Temple) to the present, a rubric for an entire
way of life. Perhaps no one has done more to bring this to the awareness of
Christians than N. T. Wright. He explains that Torah observance represented "the
covenantal charter, an unbreakable whole. It became for those living outside the

land a kind of portable land and temple in Jerusalem" (Wright 1996, 227; cf. Davies 1997, 384; Currid 2007). This practice carried right through the medieval period and continues in certain conservative branches of Judaism today.

The New Covenant

The Christian, or New Covenant, equivalent to Torah observance is living "in Christ" (Currid 2007, 68; Larsen Classnotes 2008). "Equivalent" needs to be clarified. A literal parallel does not seem to be intended, that is, following the letter of the law, which often deteriorated to zeal without commensurate understanding or faith (Rom 10:2-4). Instead, "equivalent to Torah" apparently means that the New Covenant way of life is covenantal just as there was a covenantal way of life under the older covenantal administration. In other words, all the descriptors of the Covenant in the definitions can be said to characterize the New Covenant and its consequent way of life: the very presence of God in Christ through the Holy Spirit among all covenant peoples, characterized by a *hesed* relationship on the basis of the oath established by Christ on the cross. He is our God and we are his people, bound together by the inviolable bond of his own character and word (Heb 6:13f; 7:21), as he keeps us for and in his covenantal purpose, which is always and everywhere grace and the fulfillment of his promise. Moreover, this engenders a consequent way of life that is whole life, or "world and life view" as verbalized by Abraham Kuyper (1898).

Worldview Theory and the Biblical Covenant

This second section reviews the literature on worldview theory as an equivalent to biblical covenantal theory. Worldview is the point of view of a society or individual for relating to life and reality (see definitions). Every society and individual has a worldview, and every worldview expresses a particular viewpoint. Everyone, whether cognizant or not, desires his worldview to conform as much as possible to reality, that is, he desires that it "works." Or, so say worldview theorists.

Worldview theory is the study of those viewpoints, what comprises them, how they are developed and maintained, and to what extent they correspond with reality, or gauge coherence. Christian theorists and teachers of worldview use worldview theory in much the same way, but they tend to make the effort to conform theory to their particular Christian perspective.

Is worldview theory, or the notion of worldview, taught in Scripture? Is it implied? Or, is it one of those aspects of life that is not broached in the Bible, but perhaps not taught against either? This study compares contemporary worldview theory with Scripture and asks this question: How would one defend the proposition that contemporary worldview theory functions analogously to biblical covenantal theory?

Commonalities of Worldview Theory

One can trace the language of worldview back to the German enlightenment in the late eighteenth century, although, according to some, the idea is ancient and possibly universal.[11] Worldview theory has been addressed from numerous viewpoints. Approaches in the scholarly literature include historical (Holmes 1983; Hoffecker 1986, 2007; Sire 1997; Naugle 2002); "archaeological," similar to physical anthropology (Boas 1911; Redfield 1941; Kearney 1984; Hiebert 1999a; 1999b); and structural or systems, favored by semiotics, science, and business. This section surveys key elements common to the various approaches in the literature.

One pervasive understanding is that worldview is the way individuals and societies conceptualize and classify life and reality. Michael Kearney poses the

---

11 The notion of the Transcendental Ideas *Weltbegriff* which stamp the entirety of reality, including universal categories of human reason, or unified understanding of the world *Weltganz* was a function of pure reason in Kant (*Critique of Pure Reason, Critique of Judgment*). It was later popularized especially in German literature with the word Weltanschauung or the standpoint from which one looked out at the world, somewhat in contradistinction to pure philosophy. The word was taken over into English as worldview as early as the mid nineteenth century. Before that, however, Hegel began to move the idea down the path to phenomenology. This was later supplemented by Eco's work in semiotics (see Naugle 2002, 5-16, 55-67).

classic view:

> What are the fundamental ways in which all people everywhere conceptually divide up and categorize the phenomena they perceive? Once this universal structure of world view, this meta model, is established, then the task would be to fill in the content of specific world views of different societies. (From Redfield, after Malinowski, in Kearney 1984, 37)

Kearney identifies three basic problems in worldview studies. First, what are the necessary and, therefore, universal types of images and assumptions that are part of any world view, and what are the specific contents of these universals in any particular world view? In response, he identifies seven universal categories: (1) classification, (2) relationship, (3) self, (4) other, (5) causality, (6) space, and (7) time (Kearney 1984, 43). Second, what relationship do these have with the world that they represent? According to Kearney, the answer lies in a kind of mental software (1984, 43).[12] Third, what is a worldview's influence on behavior, on practical affairs? (1984, 10).

In Kearney's comprehensive model (diagrammed by a full outer circle with interior and exterior components), worldview generates symbols and systems, which are then reified into one's sacred and geographic environment. In his conceptualization, worldview also directs outward action or behavior, coming full circle. The environment is also acted on by behavior, as well as by external sources of change. The environment, in turn, affects worldview formation and transformation (Kearney, xix, 106f).

---

12 An Idealist-Empiricist-Nominalist approach in the American cultural anthropologist school, according to Naugle and Hiebert. Hiebert notes: "If meaning is found in people's heads, then communication is measured not by the accurate transmission of objective facts, but by the inner images and feelings that are generated in the mind of the listener. Communication, therefore, must be receptor oriented. What is important is not what the sender means but what the listeners perceive" (Hiebert 1999, 41).

Paul Hiebert adapts this generally accepted theory of worldview classification categories to Christian use.[13] He accomplishes this with a model and a process. His model (figure 2) superimposes an ontological (vertical) scale: transcendence (unseen), immanence (seen), and a middle category, over a meta cultural grid of two root metaphors (organic and mechanistic) (Popper 1949), resulting in a grid of six categories (Hiebert 1999b, 45-49).

Organic	Transcendence (unseen)	Mechanistic
Organic	Middle (mixed)	Mechanistic
Organic	Immanence (seen)	Mechanistic

Figure 2. Hiebert's (religious) worldview analysis model

Hiebert utilizes this classification system in a four-step critical-realist contextualization methodology to effect worldview transformation: (1) phenomenological analysis, (2) ontological evaluation of theological criteria and reality test, (3) critical evaluation of existing beliefs, (4) missiological transformation (Ibid., 21-28). Together, these two form the core of Hiebert's Christian worldview theory.

A second important commonality in the literature is that worldview is a visualization of reality. Naugle writes: "In his book, *A Theory of Semiotics*,

---

13 Stackhouse also attempts to adapt a naturalistic alternative. "Ethology," which has roots in natural selection and anthropology, attempts, among other things, to develop speech in apes. He writes: "It is the attempt to identify which value patterns in a context, whether psychological or social, have become built into the artifactual fabric of everyday life. These patterns often determine how we assess our own worth and that of others; in addition, they frequently dominate structures of power and influence, and they delimit the available possibilities of *praxis*. Here the focus is on patterns of living, judging, and evaluating that have become 'second nature' in a context. *We seek, at this point, to understand the ethos according to its moral, spiritual, and religious qualities*" (Stackhouse 1988, 203, emphasis mine).

Umberto Eco [the principle source of semiotic theory] subsumes the entire edifice of human culture under the discipline of semiotics" (Naugle 2002, 292).[14] From the sources, it is evident that worldview is understood to be similar to a map: it is a true representation but not photographic realism.

Hiebert employs the critical-realist approach in his application of this theory:

> Signs link our mental world to the external world. They have a subjective dimension (the image in our mind), an objective dimension (the real trees to which we are referring), and a symbolic dimension (the sign, such as a word that is part of a sign system or language). . . . A triadic view of signs sees meaning not in objective realities, or in subjective mental images. Rather, it is found in the correspondence between ideas and reality mediated through sign systems. (Hiebert 199b, 72)

A third commonality in the literature is that worldview is reputed to be tacit and neutral. Edward Hall and Michael Polanyi are the most well-known exponents of the theory of worldview as tacit knowledge. Like an iceberg, "culture existed on two levels: overt culture, which is visible and easily described, and covert culture, which is not visible, and presents difficulties even to the trained observer" (Hall 1959, 64-5; from Freud, through Sapir and Kluckholm). Tacit is used by Hall as "out-of-awareness" (Ibid., 73; see Polanyi 1983, 58). Rogers appears to assume this implies that because worldview is unconscious, it is also largely biblically and morally neutral (2002).

Fourth, the literature is in general agreement that models of worldview, while not perfect, should be able to predict behavior, and vice versa. "Our *link from these abstractions to behavior* is the theoretical bias that specific world

---

14 Stackhouse summarizes the literature as "the 'science of signs' that attempts to understand the meaning of the texts in terms of their encoded logics, their function and structure in the societal context, and their performative power in generating civilizational forms and possibilities" (Stackhouse 1988, 112.

views result in certain patterns of action and not others. Therefore, knowledge of people's world view should explain aspects of their cultural behavior" (Kearney 1984, 53; emphasis mine).

From these commonalities, four assumptions that underlie these and most other contemporary worldview theories may be deduced:

1. All peoples conceptually divide up and categorize the phenomena they perceive, so that there should be an Ideal, if implicitly so, meta-cultural model of categories.

2. Life and reality are basically visually and symbolically comprehended by all peoples.

3. Because worldview is tacit, it is neutral (i.e., can be used by Christian "perspectives" (Rogers), or by any other perspective).

4. A meta-cultural type of model can be used to categorize worldview and to predict behavior, and vice versa; therefore, it can be utilized in worldview change or transformation (i.e., what Christians might refer to as conversion or sanctification, and non-theists might refer to as mechanistic or behavioristic; cf. Prv 23:7).

Contemporary Theorists Assess Worldview Assumptions

Because of the spectrum of viewpoints in worldview theory, it is crucial to understand the assumptions from which they theorize. Kearney applies his theory of universal categories to address the issue:

> What is needed is a 'reflexive anthropology of world view', or a 'meta-world view theory', exposing the ideological backgrounds that generate particular perspectives on world view and world views (Kearney 1984, x, 2; see also Jones 1972, 79).

Naugle identifies a second problem with worldview assumptions as the central problem of hermeneutics: circular reasoning, or question-begging, with thought and life proceeding on the basis of personal prejudices, particularly religious ones (Naugle 2002, 311-12), in the guise of assumptions.

A third problem of worldview assumptions is what some Christian theorists refer to as split-level living. "All Christians live between two worlds, cultural and Christian" (Hiebert 1999b, 28). The implicit admission is that these worlds may differ, resulting in compartmentalization of life with one belief system and way of living when around Christians, and another belief system for the rest of the week. He claims that split-level living has sapped the vitality of churches and limited Christianity to segments of peoples lives (Ibid., 15).

Furthermore, there appear to be real dangers associated with worldview theory thinking. First, there is the "radical objectification of reality," stemming from perceiving reality visually and by symbolic correspondence. The world and everything in it is seen as an entity to be conceived as a photograph and grasped as an object (Ibid., 332). The results are interiorization and solipsism (Ong 634, n. 2).

The postmodern critique, or "hermeneutics of suspicion" (Lyotard 1984, xxiv), renders the *coup de grâce,* placing all final interpretations of the world in doubt, including the sufficiency and authority of meta theories, such as worldview. Last, there is the danger of misrepresenting Scripture: "[T]here is great danger in speaking of the things of God in a different manner and in different terms than God himself employs" (Luther 2002, 336, n. 11; cf. Barth 2002, 335). These dangers, especially this last one, easily overlooked or treated too lightly, force a rethinking of worldview theory.

The Covenant Compared With Worldview

A willingness to rethink worldview theory provides the opportunity for searching what the Scriptures have to say in light of worldview theory. Naugle's judgment is germane:

> If it is indeed true that particular worldviews set the framework for a worldview theory, then we must inquire about the implications of a Christian worldview based on the Bible on the nature of this concept as well. (Naugle 2002, 256)

It can be determined in the literature that the biblical (Hebrew-Christian) covenant and the consequent way of life is analogous to, but radically different from, the way "worldview" is used today in the literature. In fact, the Covenant provides an equivalent to a meta-cultural model for comparing worldview assumptions, and also provides critical, or missional, engagement with other worldviews.

In the first place, the literature reveals worldview to be religious. "Our study of Western thinkers should confirm that all world views are religions" (Hoffecker 1986, 320; cf., 2000; Stackhouse 1988, 109, 113). Bavinck also points out that phenomenologically, the similarities suggest that biblical Christian faith and other religions have something in common (Bavinck 1981, 13).

1. There appears to be a fundamental unity of mankind (we are mostly alike).
2. Mankind has lived upon only a few ideas, for there are only limited choices at each juncture.
3. Humans are always answering the same questions (31).

These commonalities form the warrant for Bavinck's main proposition, his way of understanding reality from a Christian point of view:

> Therefore, it stands to reason that this universal religious consciousness is something real. . . . Is it possible to formulate the main points which have drawn the attention of man? Let us call them 'magnetic points':
>
> (1) sense of cosmic relationship: - *I and the cosmos*;
>
> (2) religious norm: - *I and the norm*;
>
> (3) between action and fate: - *I and the riddle of my existence*;
>
> (4) craving for salvation (something is wrong, and the dream of a better world): - *I and salvation*;
>
> (5) reality behind reality: - *I and the Supreme Power.* (Ibid., 32-33)

Larsen responds to this universal religious consciousness with the notion of "heart-set." Heart-set is his description of the inclination of the heart which "radically orients (or reorients [transformed by Christ]) the direction of one's thinking and culture" (Larsen 2006, 1). The natural inclination of the human heart is toward the Self and against God, against the Creator of humankind and the world. However, the "new man in Christ" is now normally oriented towards God. In his analysis, Larsen grasps three essentials of what others call worldview:

(1) Root identity: "Who am I?" Man is alone in the universe, or seeks his identity from something other than God. On the other hand, the new believer, member of the Covenant community, is now "in Christ."

(2) Core beliefs and values: "In whom do I trust?" Man relies on idols of the heart. However, the new member of the Covenant community relies on Jesus alone.

(3) Ultimate allegiance: "Whom do I obey?" Man obeys his own will, or derivative human authorities. On the other hand, the new member of the Covenant community "fears" the Lord alone. (Ibid., 2-3)

In the literature it can be seen that worldview and covenant are comparable ways to comprehend life and reality, and that they are both religious. Both Bavinck and Larsen demonstrate that there are biblical alternatives to the meta-cultural model for comparing the assumptions, beliefs, and practices that make up what is called worldview (cf. Schaeffer and Van Til).

However, as a last point, from the literature on covenant it can be understood that the biblical covenant and covenantal way of life effectively replace the old worldview for new believers and members of the covenant community (see Hoffecker and Currid, 23).

Naugle proffers this final insight on how covenant can function:

Covenant epistemology may be defined as a way of knowing that connects truth with life, that is, it recognizes that the purpose of the acquisition of knowledge is to engender obedience to the covenant that binds God and his people. Covenant epistemology means knowledge for the sake of responsible action. It connects in a radical way knowing and doing, epistemology and ethics, belief and behavior, else the consequences be hypocrisy, guilt, and personal disintegration. (Naugle 2001, 3)

Covenantal Ethnohermeneutic Theory

The literature does not contain any explicit reference to covenantal theism, or covenantal ethnohermeneutics. In and of itself, ethnohermeneutics is a rare enough topic. Consequently, the literature linking covenant to hermeneutics is in its fledgling stage. This third area of literature review explores where the biblical understanding of covenant, on one hand, overlaps with hermeneutics, the theory of context and interpretation, on the other. More precisely, it focuses on one aspect of hermeneutics: the theory of multiple horizons, or ethnohermeneutics. This smaller area of overlap entails the triadic relationship of what biblical covenant has to say to the theory of interpretation between multiple horizons or contexts: the text of Scripture, the covenant community of believers, and the unevangelized peoples of the world, or the epistemological differences between the text and different contexts. The study also explores the methodologies used to inquire about humans and human societies: what makes them "tick," and what explains differences and changes. Covenantal ethnohermeneutics asks this question of the literature: Is there a more appropriately biblical approach than exists in the literature to understanding others' worldviews and to understanding which methodologies are best suited to study them?

Because hermeneutics is the theory linking text to context[15], two questions are critical to this discussion. What are the goals of hermeneutics? What are its

---

15 Thomas Schmitz advises: "We must avoid asking a methodology to provide what it cannot provide, and we should not eschew what it can provide" (Schmitz 2007, 46). Edward Hirsch argued in *Validity in Interpretation* (1967), "the meaning of a literary text is objectively knowable, and distinguishable from the 'significance' attributed to that meaning by particular readers." In "Faulty Perspectives" (1976), Hirsch critiques the assumption that 'knowledge' is relative, coining the term 'cognitive atheism', by which he meant the notion that everybody sees

sources? First, the literature is examined for goals. Anthony Thiselton seems to reflect his generation while remaining faithful to scriptural instruction:

> The goal of biblical hermeneutics is to bring about an active and meaningful engagement between interpreter and text in such a way that the interpreter's own horizon is reshaped and enlarged."
> (Thiselton 1980, xix)

Thiselton explains that the task of hermeneutics is to educate the audience to the point that they understand what happened in the Old Testament and also with New Testament interpretation. Then, he adds, they will be able to apply the ancient text to today.

Stanford Reid links hermeneutics to both covenant and culture. He poses and then answers this pivotal question: "Can we as Christians analyse [sic] cultures, known historically, in terms of the covenant? To this question the answer must be Yes" (1954, 203).

Second, two alternative sources present themselves in the literature. The principal source for the broader cultural understanding of hermeneutics is the classical heritage from Greece. "Almost since its inception, Christian thinking about literature and culture has been governed by the categories and assumptions of the Hellenic world of the Roman Empire" (Davies 1997, 358). For most thinkers, there is no other source; it is impossible for them to conceive of other categories with which to think, so pervasive and embedded are these roots.[16]

---

literature from his own 'angle of vision', which he labels "straightforward subjectivism." Hirsch continues by identifying Herder as the originator of this relativist perspective, which Meinecke identified as 'historicism'. Hirsch highlights three consequent relativistic fallacies: (1) the inscrutable past, that is that the ancient past is unknowable, popularized by Dilthey's ditch. Gadamer and Barthes are the principle theorists today to fall in; (2) the homogeneous past, that all people of a certain age, say the Enlightenment, believed a certain way. Chief culprits who practice this false syllogism are D. W. Robinson and Bruno Snell; (3) the homogeneous present, assuming monolithic descriptions such as all, except a benighted few, hold to such and such theory. Again, Gadamer and Barthes should be noted, completing the other end of their comparative line (Hirsch 2000, 232-34).

16 Stackhouse notes this in various ways in his book *Apologia*. "We should perhaps not be surprised to find a Greek philosophical term (*praxis*) at the center of some branches of current

Historically, however, "the Jews and their religion presented a challenge to the Hellenistic assumption. Alone in that universe [*Oikoumene*] they had an alternative literature, a written tradition of comparable antiquity" (Walls 2007, 18). From Hebrew-Christian roots, then, comes an alternative source of hermeneutical understanding, that may be surprising to most. Just as surprising is the degree to which scholars, even from a Christian perspective, derive their presuppositions and categories of thought from the former in comparison with the latter.

Seven Covenantal Practices

Seven hermeneutical understandings or practices, which appear to be covenantal, emerge from the literature:

1. *Revelational.* "Only the knowledge of God gained from revelation allows us to know what is not God," what is knowledge for human endeavor, and what is crucial, saving knowledge (Davies 1997, 373). For Calvin, "the theology he brings to Scripture should be the theology he reads off of Scripture" (Edmondson 2005, 7).

2. *Hearing.* The faithful willingness to hear God's word and act upon it (i.e., begins with the *Sh'ma*, a summons more than a confession). "The willingness to hear, to understand, to cooperate [Calvin: necessitates conversion] is here declared to be the prior condition for the affirmation to which the sentence moves" (Fisch 1993, 48).

3. *Relational.* "The biblical text as a whole is founded in relationality. It demands an audience, actively participating not merely in understanding but even in constituting the text" (Fisch 1988, 48).

---

theological discussion [could also be said *of theoria, paideia,* and many more]. Christian theology in the postbiblical periods has always involved a synthesis of biblically derived symbols and philosophical modes of understanding" (Stackhouse 1988, 84). Also, "It is in any case ironically convenient that these three Greek terms [*theoria, poesis, praxis*] represent a typology of current attempts to repudiate the connection between theology and classical philosophy" [not convenient but determinative!] (Ibid., 85).

4. *Covenantal.* "The gospel must keep covenant with Torah" (Davies 375). Jesus and the New Testament writers were in covenant with the Old Testament writers. "Do we share in history, or do we reside in a history and world sundered from it [by our own ideals]?" (Edmondson 2005, 29). He asks: how can we break covenant and align ourselves with the Greeks?

5. *Righteousness.* "It . . . recognizes the role of . . . *yosher*, straightness, uprightness (Rabbi Daniel Lapin), contrasted to [classical] Christian virtue" (Davies 1997, 365).

6. *Blessing.* Common grace, wider, more inclusive than deliverance (for chosen people only) (Ibid., 373). Under the Creation ordinance and promise to Abraham, human culture is not sacred, but blessed.

7. *Fulfillment.* "The interpreter is obliged to accept the authority of the previous text but also called upon to complete its meaning" (e.g., what Matthew and the other New Testament writers did of the Old Testament) (Ibid., 370).

It needs to be acknowledged that specific references in the literature to covenantal hermeneutics, even more so ethnohermeneutics, is still in its fledgling stage. Nonetheless, this theory appears to offer much promise for relating the biblical text to ourselves and others and for understanding how others relate to reality.

Integrative Research Theory and Methodology

In social science literature one can detect a shift in what satisfies the criteria for "scientific," beginning with purely quantitative methodology (the theory that volumes of numbers approximates science), to qualitative methodology (the theory that focusing on a thick description of at least one population approximates validity), and now to integrative methodology (the theory of combining various theories and methodologies to triangulate, as a means of enhancing perspective and limiting blindspots). This study utilizes integrative research theory and methodologies for the following reasons: (1) overall design; (2) iteration; (3) warrant; (4) thick case study; (5) qualitative interviewing that allows participants to speak for themselves; (6) triangulation; and (7) development of theory.

First, overall design is critical in any inquiry. Integrative research design theory is complex, deriving theory from several perspectives. Joseph Maxwell's interactive approach is illustrative:

> Design in qualitative research is an iterative process that involves 'tacking' (Geertz 1976, 235) back and forth between the different components of design, assessing the implications of purposes, theory, research questions, methods, and validity threats for one another. Such an interactive [relational] model is more compatible with the definition of design as the arrangement of elements governing the functioning of a study than it is with design as a pre established plan for carrying out the study, or as a sequence of steps in conducting that study. (Maxwell 1996, 4)

Iteration, the second trait, is a necessary ingredient in the conduct of the research, according to Maxwell.

Others, like Robert Yin, liken design to a pre-planned blueprint that anticipates logical problems and guides the investigator through the process of collecting, analyzing, and interpreting data. "It is a *logical model of proof* that allows the researcher to draw inferences concerning causal "relations among the variables under investigation" (Nachmias & Nachmias 77-78; emphasis added).

A third strength of integrative research theory, at least as reflected in the literature, is that, for it, warrant lies in reality. John Creswell (1998) states that the strongest warrant for one's case is to have the need for it documented in the literature.

Fourth, integrative research methodology often uses the case study approach. Yin claims that the case study is a comprehensive qualitative research strategy in its own right (Yin 1994, 13). He elaborates:

A case study is an *empirical* inquiry that:

-investigates a *contemporary* phenomenon within its real-life *context*,

-especially, when the boundaries between phenomenon and context are not clearly evident [*uncontrollable*].

[Furthermore T]he case study inquiry:

-copes with the technically distinctive situation in which there will be many more variables of interest than data points, and as one result

-relies on *multiple sources* of evidence, with data needing to *converge* in a triangulating fashion, and as another result

-benefits from prior development of *theoretical* propositions to guide data collection and analysis. (Ibid., emphases mine)

Integrative research theory produces methodologies that cohere as much as possible with reality. One method is replication logic, utilized for multiple cases. Replication is employed to predict outcomes, either similar outcomes for a number of tests (a minimum of three), or to predict anomalies in which at least one test result is different (Ibid., 45). Yin advises: "Carefully select, so that it (a) predicts similar results (literal replication); or (b) produces contrasting results but for predictable reasons (theoretical replication)" (Ibid., 46).

Another methodological theory is chain of evidence. "Chain of evidence [is employed] so that an external observer (reader) can follow the derivation of evidence. Steps to accomplish this are: (a) citation; (b) location of source of citation; (c) location of actual evidence" (Ibid., 98). A third theory is concept mapping. It can be used in a variety of ways throughout the process: to develop theory; as a memo or "stickit" note; as a way of "thinking on paper"; it can show unexpected connections, or identify gaps or contradictions in one's theory and help to figure out ways to resolve the latter. To work effectively, concept mapping requires much reworking (Howard & Barton 1988, 36-42).

33

Case study methodology also has been applied to historical texts, particularly the biblical text. "The case study approach can be used to analyze a biblical character [e.g., an analysis of the character of Philemon and an inductive study of the book which bears his name]. . . . The basic objective of the case study method is to confront the student with a real life situation" (Gangel 2008).

A fifth strength of integrative research theory is qualitative interviewing, whether combined with quantitative approaches or not. "The survey questionnaire while generating useful data . . . often remains secondary . . . . Poll data sum up the private opinions of thousands of respondents. Active interviews create the possibility of public conversation and argument" (Bellah et al 1986, 305). Bellah explains further why active, or qualitative, interviewing is so rich:

> But what we were interested in above all was the language people
> used to think about their lives and the traditions from which that
> language comes. . . . In our conversations, we were listening not
> only to voices present but to voices past. In the words of those we
> talked to we heard John Calvin, Thomas Hobbes, and John Locke,
> as well as Winthrop, Franklin . . . . (Ibid., 306)

The sixth strength apparent in the literature is triangulation, which has overt history in Scripture. The "testimony of two or three witnesses" was first written over a millennium prior (Dt 19:15), and still in use in Jesus' day (Mt 18:16). "The concept of 'triangulation' from navigation methodology is applied to qualitative studies of this type in order to gain multiple perspectives and to minimize error in methodology or judgment on the part of the researcher" (Larsen 2007; cf. Calvin in Conn 1984). Types of social science triangulation are numerous, providing multiple perspectives: literature review, quantitative metrics, psychometrics, such as affective, cognitive, volitional/psychomotor/behavioral, language or semiotics, and observation, both non- and participant (Larsen 2007).

The last strength is the matter of generalizability, or external validity. Once again, Yin is carefully precise:

34

> In analytic generalizability, the investigator is striving to generalize
> a particular set of results to some broader *theory* [not to a larger
> population as in quantitative research] . . . analogous to the way a
> scientist generalizes from experimental results to theory. (Yin
> 1994, 36, emphasis mine)

Integrative research theory provides multiple interlocking and mutually complementary[17] methodological approaches. Through numerous examples in the literature, the researcher learns that, by the wise use of these tools, she can expect to (1) ground research in theory; (2) build internal validity and strengthen theory by the use of triangulation; and (3) achieve theoretical saturation.

Mutually Complementary Research Theories

While nothing in the literature directly mentions "covenantal ethnohermeneutics," nor specifically links hermeneutics to any particular research methodology, the two theories can be considered mutually complementary. Integrative research methodology and covenantal ethnohermeneutics can be mutually complementary, even if some theorists are self-avowedly naturalistic or non-biblical.

Integrative research methodology can be said to reflect biblical givens in all seven strength areas plus an eighth. In Maxwell's interactive design model of iterative tacking (1996, 4), "interactive" can be said to be relational, as in the relationality built into creation and reflected in the Covenant. Second, tacking can be said to parallel the Hebrew approach to knowing, or wisdom. Third, Creswell's demand for documented warrant (1998) takes reality seriously, as does Scripture. Fourth, Yin emphasizes a "real-life context" as the basis for case study

---

17 Complementary: can be used in at least two ways. It is denoted in the dictionary in keeping with its monist roots: adj. part of a whole, forming a complement[ary whole], from Latin (*complementum* fill up). The nominative adjective form "complementarity" provides another connotation, and is the one used in this study: mutually related, parallel, helpful, possibly overlapping, without thought of being part of a whole or completing something.

research (1994, 13) as in the biblical emphasis on concreteness. Fifth, Gangel's application of case study to ancient texts, particularly the Bible (2008), allows them to speak for themselves. Sixth, Bellah et al.'s interest in public conversation and language in qualitative interviewing (1986, 305-6) reflects biblical openness and communication of the whole truth "warts and all." Seventh, the practice of triangulation by Larsen (2007) and others illustrates biblical wisdom. Eighth, theory strengthened by actual cases and replication of cases (Creswell 1998) parallels how particular cases and givens confirm biblical universality.

In conclusion, Sibley offers this insight:

It is when we understand that interculturation involves God's accommodation, as Calvin pointed out, that we see that the intercultural process is triangular rather than merely dual (God, the covenant community, and the unevangelized community). (2004, 7)

These eight methodological theories comprise a body of scientific research methodology that reflects this relationship between biblical-creational design and sound human practice.

CHAPTER 3

RESEARCH DESIGN

Purpose and Design

The purpose of the research portion of the study is to explore the research concerns, to test the research questions in actual real-world cases, and to develop theory, in this particular instance, about the Covenant and covenantal theism, or ethnohermeneutics. A well-designed research methodology should achieve a high degree of correspondence or triangulation between actual cases, research questions and theory, both precedent and developing.

The overall research question investigated in this study is: What is the role of the Ten Commandments in discipling the nations? Five subsidiary questions are asked of three cultural scenes or case studies: (1) What/who is the focus of the case study? (2) What does the transcript itself report of the participants' former way of life (worldview), and what covenantal instruction from the Ten Words is needed? (3) What does the Covenant entail, of what does the covenantal way of life consist, and how is this new way different from their old way of life? (4) By what means are the Ten Words used to instruct the participants? (5) To what extent are the Covenant or the Ten Words used to instruct the participants and in what ways are they instruments of grace?

The two mutually complementary theory areas of covenantal theism or covenantal ethnohermeneutic theory, and integrative and qualitative research methodology theory, govern the conduct of research and analysis for this study. First, it is reflected in the overall design. Among the multitude of qualitative approaches, this study relies primarily on the Case Study. Because of its real-world setting (Yin 1994, 13), case study methodology is a powerful tool of analysis due to two primary strengths: (1) holistic, in-depth investigation (Feagin,

Orum, & Sjoberg, 1991), and (2) triangulated research strategy.[18] Case study methodology can also be said to parallel the biblical emphasis on real-life contexts.

Data Sources and Types

Data sources and types are triangulated between two case studies based upon exegesis and content analysis of biblical literature (Bauman 1995; Krippendorf 1980; Lovejoy 1936; Nisbet 1969; Schafer 1980; Weber 1990; Wells 1998; Gangel 2008) and a contemporary case study of two related cultural scenes in twenty-first- century America (Yin 1994; Maxwell 1996) based upon qualitative field interviews (Bellah *et al* 1984; Rubin and Rubin 1995), utilizing a blind, open-ended questionnaire employing the critical power of the Ten Words .

Methodology

A research protocol guides methodology applied to the three case studies utilized in this study, analysis of the data, and report of the findings:

1. Design
    a. Determine and define research questions
    b. Select the case(s)/identify population(s)
    c. Determine data gathering and analysis techniques
    d. Determine, craft, and test protocol itself
2. Conduct qualitative interview
    a. Craft and test instrument(s)
    b. "Interview" ancient text transcripts
    c. Apply questionnaire to contemporary respondents

18 The need for triangulation arises from the ethical need to confirm the validity of the sources and processes. In case studies, this could be done by using multiple sources of data (Yin, 1994).

3. Conduct case studies

    a. Prepare and collect data

    b. Protect chain of evidence

    c. Using concept mapping, tack iteratively between design, collection, analyses and literature (theory)

4. Analyze and triangulate

    a. Analyze utilizing qualitative and quantitative methods

    b. Conduct within-case analyses

    c. Compare cross-case replication with other cases

    d. Consult literature (theory)

5. Reach closure: develop conclusions, recommendations, and implications based on the findings:

    a. Summarize findings

    b. Derive conclusions and formulate theory

    c. Explore implications, including replication

    d. Make recommendations

6. Prepare and write the report. (adapted from Simons 1980; Yin 1994; Stake 1995)

Data Analysis

One of the real strengths of the integrative approach is the combination of quantitative and qualitative methods, and the use of triangulation. When data have been gathered from the three data pools, a three-step process of comparative analysis ensues (Eisenhardt 1989; Collier and Mahan 1993; Gall, Gall & Borg 2003; Mahoney and Rueschemeyer 2003). First, the findings are analyzed within each case, by methods germane to the type. Textual, content, and historical analyses are applied to the two biblical cases. Rasch-type quantitative analysis, simple statistical analysis, qualitative (covenantal), and critical (Agar 1991) analyses are applied to the contemporary case). Second, the findings are compared and analyzed across the cases for the three to determine actual or theoretical replication, if any. Then, these are cross checked with theory from precedent literature to note continuities and anomalies.

CHAPTER 4

CASE ONE: THE LIBERATION OF ISRAEL AS A NATION AND THE RENEWAL OF THE COVENANT UNDER MOSES

Introduction

Around 1400 B.C. a large people group suddenly emerged from Egypt and moved en masse across the Sinai peninsula to the neighboring area of Palestine. The chief significance of this episode is that it happened--it is not a fantastical fable or a conjectured reconstruction of mythical events. Through a theophanic deliverance and covenantal enactment, God delivered the people of Israel and reconstituted them as a nation.

The Jewish people look to that episode as the founding event of what is today a universal religious community, and memorialize it annually. Likewise, the worldwide Christian community looks to it through the key Jewish descendant, Jesus Christ. New believers are still being inducted and becoming functioning members, and Jesus Christ promised to come again to complete the story.

This is a case study of that foundational event, including its unique covenantal constitution. It is organized as follows:

1. Introduction.

   a. Introductory material and significance

   b. Outline

   c. Case study methodology

2. Analysis and Findings.

   a. Brief summary of the original "transcript" of the biblical text

   b. The setting for the event

   c. Fabric of the context: historical, geographical, cultural, literary, and observations from the legal text

d.   The next step--the Mosaic Covenant, including how the Ten Words were employed

3.   Conclusions, implications, and recommendations.

Despite the skepticism of some scholars regarding both the historicity and relevance of the Sinai event after such a lengthy gap of time, this paper takes the position of most conservative Jewish and Christian scholars that (1) the event was sufficiently noted orally and in written sources to communicate everything God intended for that generation and future ones; and that (2) Hebrew history is, in any case, written as a descriptive, finished work, mostly directed towards the future, rather than in order to seek moral lessons from recurrent patterns in the past, as in the case of Greek historiography (Maggiotto 1997; Harrison 1970, 300).

A thick case study provides an explicit retelling of the lives and culture of an actual people group at a specific time and place.

Case: The Mosaic Covenant—God's liberation of Israel from Egypt to Canaan, and the renewal of his moribund covenant with them, including the enactment of the "Ten Words"—the Mosaic Instructions.

Research question (RQ): By what means and to what extent were the Ten Words (Commandments) used to lead the children of Israel to the covenantal way of life, or to become functioning members of the covenant community?

Sources: The biblical text (the biblical books of Moses, specifically, Ex 19-20, 24) is used in this study as the 'transcript', as such, of the original event. It is purported to have been written or compiled by Moses[19] at the time of the

---

19 The debate continues whether at least one version of this material (Exodus) can be legitimately attributed to Moses, or whether the entire collection is a late (post-exilic) redaction of disparate traditions from various periods of Israel's history. A credible scholarly tradition (Albright, Cassuto, Glueck, Harrison, Speiser, among others) considers Moses the author-editor of the Bible's first five books, four of which elaborate this episode and its immediate aftermath (Cassuto, 1972, 1-6, 12). Numerous references to other writings, sayings, and sagas, poems and other oral stories from this period, not contained in the text attributed to him, are cited throughout the Hebrew Bible. Other scholars (particularly Martin Noth and his students) argue that the importance of these books is how they function within the Israelite society of the Iron Age [which, in itself, presupposes a prior date!] (Halsall 2001).

incident, and provides the primary source material.[20] Secondary literature is consulted, as well.

Brief Summary of the Text

Due to a severe region-wide famine, seventy or so members of one pastoral, possibly bedouin-type, clan from Canaan settled in Egypt approximately 3800 years ago. They were welcomed with open arms because one of their number, Joseph, originally sold as a slave into Egypt, had risen, due to God's providential blessing and his vision and wise superintendence, to rescue the whole nation of Egypt from the consequences of a famine. Israel's clan was settled in a fertile border area, possibly because of Egyptian taboos regarding their animal husbandry.

Why they stayed after harvests returned remains unclear. Perhaps they found abundant resources to prosper and multiply, as they did "exceedingly" (Ex 1:7). Over time, in fact, the Israelites grew so numerous that the Egyptian authorities felt threatened and sought to entrap them into a position of subjugation.[21] After an indeterminate time of forced indentureship, their misery prompted God to rescue them.

This he accomplished in supernatural fashion through the reluctant leadership of Moses and his elder brother and spokesman, Aaron. God sprang the

---

20 This author assumes divine inspiration for the biblical text, which is the primary source for this case study per its own self definition of inspiration (2 Pt 1:16-21). It is therefore absolutely authoritative. That said, he also recognizes that the actual population is no longer available, and that the text can be used as the transcript of the primary research conducted at the time of the event or shortly thereafter. Therefore, it is this text and not the actual episode that will be mined for clues and data, as is similarly the case in all historical research.

21 "A new king, who did not know about Joseph, came to power in Egypt. 'Look,' he said to his people, 'the Israelites have become much too numerous for us. Come, we must deal shrewdly with them or they will become even more numerous and, if war breaks out, will join our enemies, fight against us and leave the country.' So they put slave masters over them to oppress them with forced labor, and they built Pithom and Rameses" (Ex 1:8). It can be argued that this new king was probably the first of the foreign Hyksos (proto-Assyrian?) to rule Egypt (15th dynasty 1600-1500). If so, they may have harbored a historical antipathy to the Jews. In any case, they subjugated them and forced them to build the royal city of Rameses to honor the Hyksos (Wood 1998).

Egyptian trap by the humiliation of their divine lord Pharaoh, [22] the embodiment of all the powers of nature by which the Egyptians had built up such a rich and powerful nation and maintained it, dynasty after dynasty. He stripped them of Pharaoh's subterfuge of divinity, of the slave-labor upon which the rulers built their position of wealth and power, and even of some of the material wealth possessed by their upper caste. Following a series of supernatural devastations of Egyptian patrimony, including even the loss of the firstborn (strength) of all humans and livestock, as many as one million Israelites are reported to have quickly mobilized and hurried away in orderly fashion "in full view of all the Egyptians who were burying their firstborn" (Nm 33:3-4) to worship God in the desert.

In the next few days the Israelites were forced into a terrifying brand of hide-and-seek with the belatedly regretful Egyptian army. They were rescued once again in dramatic fashion over a dry pathway through open water, then they were tested over whether they could trust God's deliverance to continue, to the point of daily sustenance, in what seemed an empty wilderness. Finally, they were ordered to encamp and purify themselves to meet with the living God at the foot of Mount Sinai.

Listen to the transcript of this encounter directly from eyewitnesses:
On the morning of the third day [after the people began consecrating themselves] there were thunders and lightnings and a thick cloud on the mountain and a very loud trumpet blasting, so that all the people in the camp trembled. Then Moses brought the people out of the camp to meet God, and they all stood their ground at the foot of the mountain. Now Mount Sinai was wrapped in smoke because the Lord had descended on it in fire. The smoke of it went up like the smoke of a kiln, and the whole mountain shook violently. And as the sound of the trumpet grew

22 Who, if Hyksos, was already an impostor: an Asian acting as the Egyptian pharaoh.

louder and louder. . . . the Lord came down on Mount Sinai, to the top of the mountain . . . . And God spoke all these words [in thunder], saying:

"I AM the LORD your GOD who brought you out of the land of Egypt, from the house of slavery.

HAVE NO OTHER GODS BUT ME.

DO NOT MAKE OR WORSHIP IMAGES/ICONS OF ME. For I the LORD your God am a jealous god, visiting the sins of the fathers on the children to the third and fourth generation of those who despise me, but showing loyal love to thousands of those who love me and keep my words.

DO NOT USE MY NAME, THE LORD YOUR GOD, IN VAIN, for I will not hold him guiltless.

REMEMBER TO SET THE SABBATH DAY APART. Six days you shall labor, and do all your work, but the seventh day is a sabbath to the LORD your GOD. On it you shall not do any work, you, or your sons or daughters, or your servants, or your livestock or your sojourners in your midst. For in six days the LORD made heaven and earth, the sea, and all that is in them, and rested the seventh day. Therefore the LORD blessed the Sabbath day and set it apart.

HONOR YOUR FATHER AND MOTHER, that your days may be long in the land that the LORD your GOD is giving you.

DO NOT MURDER.

DO NOT FORNICATE/COMMIT ADULTERY.

DO NOT STEAL.

DO NOT LIE/GIVE FALSE TESTIMONY AGAINST YOUR NEIGHBOR.

DO NOT COVET ANYTHING OF YOUR NEIGHBOR'S: his

house, wife, servants, animals or anything else that is your
neighbor's."

Now, when all the people saw the thunder and the flashes of
lightning and the sound of the trumpet, and the mountain smoking,
the people were afraid and trembled, and they distanced
themselves . . . . while Moses approached the thick darkness
where God was. (Exo 19:16-19; 20:1-21; author's translation)

In order to augment understanding of the actuality and specificity in time
and space of the Israelite culture, and its significance for today, this paper
examines the written clues to the complex drama that unfolded in the desert.
First, the setting, and then the rich cultural fabric are examined.

Setting

An easily missed phrase in the grand sweep of this story of liberation and
covenant provides the clue to the broader setting. After briefly describing the
plight of the Israelites and introducing Moses, the main human protagonist, the
text states:

During that long period, the king of Egypt died. The Israelites
groaned in their slavery and cried out, and their cry for help . . .
went up to God. God heard their groaning and *He remembered his
covenant* with Abraham, with Isaac and with Jacob. So, God
looked on the Israelites and was concerned about them. (Ex 2:23-
25; emphasis added)

Rather than a series of unintended consequences or reactions to
circumstances that befell the Israelites, everything pertaining to this episode was
according to God's stated purpose and plan. When he originally made the
covenant with Abraham, their first patriarch in Canaan more than five hundred
years earlier, he had declared:

Know for certain that your descendants will be strangers in a
country not their own, and they will be enslaved and mistreated

four hundred years. But I will punish the nation they serve as slaves, and afterward they will come out with great possessions. You, however, will go to your fathers in peace and be buried at a good old age. In the fourth generation your descendants will come back here, for the sin of the Amorites has not yet reached its full measure. (Gn 15:13-16)

This story was surely passed down from father to son, from Abraham to Isaac, from Isaac to Jacob, and from Jacob to his sons. Joseph must have recalled the promise when he told his brothers, who had sold him into slavery in Egypt and at the death of their father, Jacob, were afraid of Joseph's revenge: "Don't be afraid. Am I in the place of God? You intended to harm me, but God intended it for good to accomplish what is now being done, the saving of many lives" (Gn 50:15-21). Joseph realized two truths about God's covenant promise: (1) all that was happening to him and the Israelites was according to God's purpose and plan; (2) God meant them good by it, not harm. Everything that happened was for their benefit.

It can be argued that the setting for all that ensued was God's covenant promise to preserve Abraham's seed down through the generations and various circumstances of their lives. Just as their rescue from famine was due to the enslavement of Joseph, so the years of harsh slavery, the exodus from Egypt, the Sinai episode, and the wilderness wanderings full of doubt and fear also somehow set the stage for the renewal of the Covenant through Moses.

Fabric of the Context

Having surveyed the setting, it is time to turn to the actual cultural scene. The spare indications in the primary texts of the existence of an Israelite culture about the time of the Exodus and covenant renewal immediately following, confirm that the community of Israel exhibited most of the characteristics common to functioning societies. It is unreasonable to suppose that this people

48

existed with this level of cultural organization for several generations without having carried on and developed culture, laws (if informal), and institutions to support an advanced level of social organization. The layers of such a thick description are multiple: history, culture, geography, literature, revelation (for biblical cases), and covenant-law. The following sections describe the warp and woof of that cultural fabric.

History

The community of Israel in Egypt could trace its history back over four hundred years to origins in Mesopotamia. To establish his bona fides, Moses' lineage is mentioned three times (Ex 1:1-5; 2:1; 6:13-27). Lineage may have existed in written records, but was certainly and carefully passed down orally from father to son. Each family and tribe kept a record of their lineage lines down through the generations, in the manner crucial to tribal societies throughout the world (figure 3).

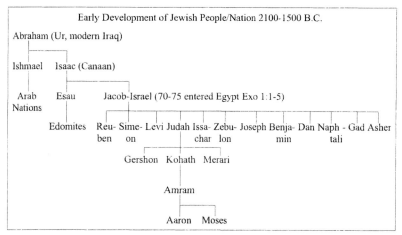

Figure 3. Lineage of Moses. Each reported generation may represent more than one actual generation (1 Chr 1:28-2:1).

49

Culture

It is reasonable to assume that the community had a commensurate complexity of language, traditions, probability structures, beliefs, and rituals, social organization, and institutions such as any culture at a similar stage of development might possess. Joel Rosenberg underscores: "These works [Hebrew biblical texts] generated a cultural legacy" (Holtz 1984, 31). The questions arise: what kind and to what extent?

From clues in the biblical text, we know they spoke a common language (Ex 4:29-31). They almost certainly possessed writing at a degree of sophistication (Ex 17:14; 24:7; 34:27; Nm 5:23; Dt 27:3; 31:19), as did other Semitic groups of the time.

Socially, they functioned under a system of elders (Ex 4:29-31; 18:13-27) (Cassuto 1987, 40). The eldest of each family, clan, and tribe, oversaw, was responsible for, and authoritative over, his group. His word was law, and together with other elders, he practiced a group decision-making process for the tribe or entire group, much as has also been commonly practiced in tribal groups throughout recorded time, and, for example, is practiced by Semitic Bedouins today.

Religiously, the Israelite community knew a common name for God (*El Shaddai* God Almighty) and had a "fear" or awe of him, at least some did (Ex 1:17; 3:13-15). In this scene, they learned a new name: the untranslatable *Yahweh*, but they used the designation Lord. They were not unduly surprised with visions or messages that certain people reportedly received from this God (Ex 3:16-18; 4:27-28). It is reasonable to assume probable common rituals such as circumcision and burial rites (Ex 13:19).

As for social organization, a midwife system functioned to ensure natality, sufficiently organized to have two representatives liaising with the Egyptian authorities (Ex 1:15-19). The Israelites were known for their animal husbandry, and trading raw wools and hides, and probably the millinery and artisan trades associated with these, and so on (Gn 46:31-47:6).

The level of social fabric and organization appears sufficient to provide a distinct identity throughout their time in Egypt. It was able to withstand, to some degree, the harsh slavery into which they had been entrapped, and reasserted itself quickly enough so that within a few days time they were able to (1) enact the *Pascha,* a new community-wide celebration of their release including marking the doorways to escape divine judgment, (2) "despoil" their Egyptian neighbors, [23] and (3) mobilize upwards of a million people to leave with their belongings (Ex 12).

Geography

The Israelites kept such detailed records of geographic markers and dates that people today could trace their exact route if place designations of the time[24] were known today (Nm 33; the entire chapter is devoted to detailing the more than thirty stages of Israel's journey from Egypt to Canaan).

Such records were kept, most certainly in written form, providing yet another clue as to the cultural values and degree of cultural sophistication at that time. More than likely, records were not compiled from amateur observations but were kept and maintained by a kind of guild whose role it was in the Israelite social order to perform such tasks. Perhaps they learned the craft from the Egyptians, who were also inveterate record keepers regarding the divinity (Pharaohship). These questions remain unanswered. Nevertheless, their efforts described for that, and succeeding generations, the very real context for their escape, covenant renewal, implementation of a new cult, fight for survival in

---

23 The language of the text ("ask their [Egyptian] neighbors [friend/acquaintance]" Ex 11:2; "nearest [Israelite] neighbor [next door/nearby inhabitant]" 12:4 is inconclusive whether the Israelites were herded into a ghetto, but unmistakable that they had acquaintances among wealthy Egyptians.

24 The place designations may actually be ones recognizable to a somewhat later generation of readers than the actual Exodus. Rameses is a fairly known case in point, estimated to have been built as a royal city a century or so after the date of the Exodus.

the spare wasteland conditions and against various other people groups who sought their harm, and their wanderings.

Literature

The most important thing to note is that we are able to discuss the Hebrew literature of that period at all. The repeated efforts of many erudite scholars throughout the nineteenth and early twentieth centuries to call into question whether written Hebrew existed at this early point have been almost silenced by subsequent archaeological discoveries and careful analysis.

Owing to the age of the Torah, and because the Hebrew Scriptures were originally a book to be read aloud for the instruction of the common people (Ex 24:7; Dt 31:11), its language is that of concrete description. Its truths "could not be stated in abstract terms, simply as a theoretical concept. . ." (Cassuto 1961, 12, 71). To approach biblical narrative is to "confront a rich interweave of modes" (Holtz 1984, 34), many distinctly Middle Eastern, and some foreign to the Western reader. Important literary devices liberally used in the text include wordplay, under- and over-statement, selectivity of narrative, the marker *waw* to link narrative sections, *inclusio* to "bookend" particular sections, and deliberate ambiguity, to name a few.

Mining The Text

Finally, we turn to mining clues in the text itself. What the people did and how they behaved during the extremely stressful time in question reveals something of their character, their culture, what is termed "worldview" today, and so on. A fruitful study is to conduct a kind of reverse engineering [25] from God's

---

[25] Reverse engineering begins with a finished product or technology, and works backward to recreate the engineering concepts by analyzing the design of the system and the interrelationships of its components, so as to ascertain how it was designed or how it operates, in order to reproduce it precisely or to address some problem (taken from Frequently Asked Questions about Reverse Engineering; available at www.chillingeffects.org/reverse/faq.cgi). As applied to content analysis, it describes the process of deducing from explicit textual clues to approximate a social, cultural, and psychological profile, for example.

revealed case laws and legal commentary to the kinds of behaviors and attitudes that these laws must have been designed to limit as *not* fitting for covenant people. Some of these can be seen in the text, and others only can be surmised.

The diversity of words used for the people's responses during these intense trials and the times mentioned are remarkable: impatience (*qatsar*) 1x, sigh or moan (*'anach*) 1x, groan (*nehawkaw*) 2x, complain (*'anan*) 1x, quarrel (*riyb*) 6x, grumble or murmur (*luwn*) 18x, and the most common: cry out (*za'aq*) 1x, cry (*tsa'aq*) 15x and (*shav'aw*) 1x, and weep bitterly (*bakah*) 13x.

The Lord's grievance list is long regarding the Israelites: they almost certainly worshiped other gods in Egypt (Ex 32:8; Lv 18:3; Ez 20:5-8); they engaged in improper sexual relations (Lv 18), even according to the standards of other Semitic law codes; they would rather return to Egypt than accept God's leading (Ex 16:3; 17:3; Nm 11:20; 14:1-4; 20:5; 21:5; Dt 1:27); they learned "other ways" (cultural mores) (Lv 18:3; 20); they let rebellious sons infect the rest of the community (Deu 21:18-21); having just been freed from slavery themselves, they indentured others, so common was the practice (Dt 23:15); they were unfaithful and disobedient (Dt 28:15). Moreover, the Israelites were full of cravings during times of testing and in relation to the everyday sameness of the manna, even if miraculous (Nm 11:4f). The Lord said of them that they were "stiff-necked" (Dt 10:16), "set on evil" (Ex 32:22), and that everyone "did what was right in their own eyes" (Dt 12:8).

The list is just as long of things that they failed to do, a surmise based on the case law conditions: making covenants or treaties with others; keeping clean, especially with regard to foods and bodily wastes; perverting worship; malicious witnesses; disrespecting females, especially slaves; charging onerous interest; using double standards even in dealing with each other; pilfering; and divorcing, to name the more overt.

At the same time, some positive characteristics are noted. We know, for example, that although the midwives were ordered to perform infanticide, presumably under the threat of execution for themselves, they "feared God" more than Pharaoh (Ex 1:17), with absolutely no indication in the text of any overt religious support system. Also, from the almost complete silence regarding circumcision, it is probable that Israel maintained the practice during its stay in Egypt (Ex 4:24). Later, in the wilderness, these people could learn songs of praise from Moses, and Miriam imitated Moses by composing a song to the Lord (Ex 15). Texts also indicate that they were generous, whether unusually or habitually (Ex 36), that they had good intentions to obey the Lord (Ex 19:8; 24:3, 7; Dt 5:27; 26:17), and that they (at least Moses) "connected the dots" between God's past deliverance and his future deliverance in the Promised Land (Ex 15:14-18).

In short, the Israelites do not seem remarkably different from what one would expect of most people groups, with the exception of two primary responses. The first outstanding character quality was their seemingly unexpected generosity, in the midst of all the uncertainty and deprivation, in donating what they had to build the tabernacle (Ex 36). On the other hand, their primary response to every new situation seems to have been fear and unbelief. The writer of the Book to the Hebrews of the New Testament, in particular, cites their unbelief or disobedience as God's singular criteria for determining blessings or curses, life or death.

The Mosaic Covenant

At last the case study arrives at the acme of the text: the theophany, renewing of the Covenant, and giving the Ten Words (Ex 19:1-20:21). The whole episode came to be recognized as the most important event in Judaism and one of the most significant events in human history. For the purposes of this study, it is called the Mosaic Covenant, or Mosaic Instructions (this section is taken primarily from Averbeck and Currid).

God is the Focus

A prima facie reading might lead to the conclusion that this story, this cultural scene, is about the Law of God, or possibly about the Mosaic Covenant. Actually, the evidence suggests that it is about God. This is his scene, what has become popularly known as a "God-event," that is, the direct involvement of God in human history, not merely through secondary causes or means. God is the central personality, he initiates the Covenant and all other activity, he enacts the Ten Words into law, and he concludes the matter--the covenant enactment.

God is mentioned more than twice as many times (63) as the leading human protagonist Moses (31). The section begins with the Lord summoning Moses (Ex 19:3); his first words are: "You yourselves saw what I did to Egypt, and how I carried you (away) . . . . all the world is mine" (Ex 19:4-5); the Ten Words begin similarly: "And God spoke all these words: 'I am the Lord your God who brought you out of the land of Egypt, out of the land of slavery. You shall have no other gods'" (Ex 20:1-3); and the section concludes with: "You yourselves saw that I spoke (directly) to you from heaven . . . . make Me an altar" (Ex 20:22, 24), probably indicating another *inclusio*, possibly indicating the importance of signs that this was God's direct doing, start to finish.

The Covenantal Structure of the Scene

The transcript of this cultural scene appears to be structured as an enactment of an ancient Near Eastern covenant. "Recent research shows that covenant pervades the Old Testament and its world on several levels" (Averbeck 116). In the biblical context, "covenant" appears to define how parties that were not naturally related (by blood), related long-term to one another.[26] Covenant was used in personal matters (Gn 44), for Hittite war treaties (Mendenhall 1954, 1955;

---

26 Cf. Davidson 1989, 324. "In the Old Testament and ancient Near East 'to make a covenant' encompassed not one but two basic ideas: stipulation and oath" (Baltzer 1971, 16); cf. McCarthy 1981, 140; and esp. Weinfeld 1973, 190.

Kline 1968; Weinfeld 1973), and most importantly and possibly paradigmatically, for the covenant between the God of the Bible and his chosen people.

The covenantal renewal process appears to have been conducted in a manner familiar to the Israelites. Scholars have uncovered similarities, and possible precedents, to specific customs such as Hittite treaties, Mesopotamian royal grants, ancient Near East loyalty oaths, and law collections, such as Hammurabi's.

Averbeck outlines the process. It began with the Lord's preliminary announcement of a covenant relationship with Israel:

> The Lord called to Moses from the mountain and said, "This is what you are to say to the house of Jacob and what you are to tell the people of Israel: 'You yourselves have seen what I did to Egypt, and how I carried you on eagles' wings and brought you to myself. Now if you obey me fully and keep my covenant, then out of all nations you will be my treasured possession. Although the whole earth is mine, you will be for me a holy nation.' These are the words you are to speak to the Israelites." (Ex 19:3-6)

Next, Israel proclaimed their initial acceptance by oath, of the covenant that the Lord had enacted, in the probable context of a fellowship meal: "So Moses went back and summoned the elders of the people and set before them all the words the Lord had commanded him to speak. The people all responded together, 'We will do everything the Lord has said'" (Ex 19:7-8).

After the appropriate preparations had been made and precautions had been taken (see Ex 19:9-15), the Lord proclaimed his lordship in theophanic wonders and by self-pronouncement (Ex 19:16-20:2), followed by his "stipulations" (Ex 20:2-17), the parameters of the covenant: the Ten Words.

At this point the transcript appears to be interrupted: first the people's emotional response to the theophany is noted. Then there is the conclusion of what appears to be an *inclusio* ("You saw . . . You saw", Ex 19:4 and 20:22), without, however, the concluding fellowship meal and oath. The best explanation seems to be the Hebrew penchant for a kind of *non sequitur* in the narrative in which a matter raised in the text is dealt with immediately, before continuing with the narrative (Rosenberg 41f), in this case rules anticipating their natural desire to build him an altar and rules concerning the treatment of slaves and justice and mercy in general, since this was the Israelites' immediate prior context. The rest of the 613 'case laws' were given following the covenant has been solemnized.

When the transcript resumes, God and Israel solemnized the covenant commitment, with the leadership of Israel proclaiming an oath, and again celebrating a fellowship meal together:

> When Moses went and told the people all the Lord's words and laws, they responded with one voice, "Everything the Lord has said we will do" (Ex 24:3); Then the Lord said to Moses, "Come up to the Lord, you and Aaron, Nadab and Abihu, and seventy of the elders of Israel." . . . Then Moses and Aaron, Nadab and Abihu and the seventy elders of Israel went up and saw the God of Israel. . . . and they ate and drank. (Ex 24:1, 9, 11) (Averbeck 1995, 117-8)

Some biblical theologians might perceive a salvation-historical process in the scene structure (see figure 4):

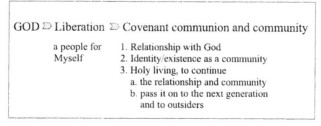

Figure 4. Salvation history process

The Covenant and the Ten Words (Law)

The laws or instructions in the Pentateuch are connected to the covenantal bonds and agreements that were made between God, the sovereign Lord, and Israel, his subject people. Averbeck writes: "Without covenant there is no law [instructions]" (Averbeck 1995, 134). At least, "The Bible itself does not conceive of a law code without a covenant at its base" (Weinfeld 1973, 273). More precisely, the Ten Words appear to parallel the function of stipulations in Ancient Near Eastern treaties. Thus, we can say that they appear to be "instructional stipulations." Through their acceptance of the covenant, the Israelites understood that they were now responsible to observe these instructions (Ex 19:4-8; 24:3-8; Dt 5:1-5; 26:16-27:8).

The Uniqueness of the Ten Words

Although parallels of the Ten Words (and consequent collection of case laws) can be demonstrated with other ancient Near Eastern codes of law, [27] and even with moral codes as distant as that of Confucius, nevertheless, it is also true that "the context and text of the Ten Commandments are unlike any other moral code or legal document" (Clowney 2007, 2). What other people received their laws directly from their deity?[28] What other deity spoke directly in an audible

---

[27] The Ancient Near Eastern background to the Ten Words: Douma writes: "From extra-biblical sources, we know that during this period, other nations also used tablets for establishing a covenant" (Douma 1992, 1). Other scholars concur: "The parallels between the laws of Hammurabi and biblical law are obvious and important, but not exact. When the Lord introduced the law for his people he often used categories and provisions of law that would have been very familiar to the people before the revelation at Sinai" (Averbeck 1995, 129; cf. also Wiseman 1962, 166). These include 'edicts' (temporary one-time selective righting of disruptive influences built up over time), law collections (relatively comprehensive and standing for extended periods of time), and ritual legislation (governing cult activity and purpose, including purity or washings laws). Kline (1963) and others have said that the Ten Words are the "stipulations" of the Covenant or are an ancient Near Eastern "law code," albeit unique .

[28] Muhammad claimed to receive his privately. Unlike the tradition of oracles in most ancient societies, God spoke in an audible voice directly to all the Israelites without any mediation (Ex 20:1). Later, it is said that he also wrote the Ten Words with his finger directly on the stone tablets that he asked Moses to bring up on the mountain (Ex 31:18). That this kind of direct

voice to the people or wrote them in stone with his finger? This speaks of "paramount importance" and also uniqueness from the human viewpoint and "[with]in the divine government" (Pink 1974, 5-6). Furthermore, the structure of the Mosaic Covenant is unique. The biblical covenants differ from other ancient Near Eastern treaties in that no evidence exists that their stipulations ever became the basis for law collections, as did the Ten Words.

Various words are used for what God thundered and wrote from Mt. Sinai--the Covenant, Mosaic, "Law." The first and most basic term was "word" (דָּבָר *dabar*): "God spoke these words," "the words of the covenant," and "the ten words" (Ex 34:28; Dt 4:13; 10:4). Other more specific terms used are: "ordinance," literally judgment (מִשְׁפָּט *mishpat*), later classified as casuistic or case law (working out or enlarging the ten "apodictic" words); "command" (מִצְוָה *mitzvah*); "statute" (חֹק *khoq*); and "instruction" (תּוֹרָה *torah*). "Precise lines of division [identifying 'decree' with apodictic and 'ordinance' with casuistic] do not reflect the way the terminology and the laws themselves are mixed in the various Old Testament law collections" (Averbeck 1995, 121) (Lv 26:46).

Immediately following Moses' death, the most common designation for the Ten Words and consequent case laws became "the instruction (*torah*) of Moses," (Jos 8:31, 32, 22:5, 23:6). This continued throughout the Old Testament period to the post-exilic books, (Ezr 3:2, 7:6; Neh 8:1, 10:29), and into New Testament times (Jn 7:23, Acts 15:5; Paul in Acts 13:34; 1 Cor 9:9), including also the lone Gentile author (Lk 2:22, 24:44). At some point the instruction of Moses became understood as the law of Moses, possibly during the intertestamental period.

---

revelation from the deity is noted only once in Scripture (until the advent of *Messiah*) indicates its extreme importance.

The Role of the Ten Words in Helping New
Believers Become Functioning Members of the Covenant Community

God provided the Mosaic instructions in order to illustrate what he considered necessary to their newly revived covenant relationship, and to serve as his divine commentary for the development of their renewed nationhood. [29] What was God's plan through Moses to accomplish this? Given the hostile situation of extreme deprivation and hostile enemies, with strong-willed people who always went their own way, were bent on sinning, and were characterized by fear and unbelief, how would God lead them in his ways?

At the core of his plan lay the Ten Words, which were used to enculturate the Israelites to become functioning members of the covenant community. "The structure and content of the Ten Commandments demonstrate and underscore their peculiarly binding character upon the people of Israel" (Currid 2001, 33) in four ways: First, the first four commandments set forth man's relationship to God, and the remaining six outline man's relationship to his fellow man. Second, when God revealed the Ten Commandments he spoke from the first to the second person singular: "I . . . you." In other words, he addressed the nation as a whole on a personal basis. "That singular form highlights the covenantal oneness of the people of God, and it emphasizes the binding nature of the commandments upon the entire nation." Third, the number "ten" in Hebrew often symbolizes completeness, meaning that no additions are allowed. And fourth, the commandments were written on both sides of the stone tablets, covering them completely, leaving no room for additions (Ex 32: 15) (Currid 2001, 33; Kline 1963).

---

29 Cassuto forcefully argues that the Mosaic instructions were given by God to serve judges and rulers as authoritative commentary as they enacted and decided law, *not* the actual laws themselves. This was based on the historic exigency of already having laws, the relative incompleteness of the Mosaic instructions, the relative lack of their actual observance, the occurrence of laws promulgated throughout the kingship apart from the Mosaic instructions, and the use of *Torah* as the general label, unlike words in other Semitic cultures for their law codes and collections (Cassuto 1987, 260-62ff; Kaiser 1987, 164.

Upon closer examination, these textual observations provide clues that the Ten Words were God's instruments of grace, instructional stipulations. As such they (1) were accompanied by signs of his deity, (2) taught what God was like and what He was not like, (3) tested the people, (4) created a promise of hope, (5) provided parameters for a covenant people, (6) explicated what loving God only and loving your neighbor as yourself, involves, and (7) instructed in such a way as to teach others (their children and the nations).

God first gave signs[30] of his deity and of his deliverance from Mt. Sinai:

On the morning of the third day [after the people began consecrating themselves] there was thundering and lightning and a thick cloud on the mountain and a very loud trumpet blasting, so that all the people in the camp trembled. Then Moses brought the people out of the camp to meet God, and they all stood their ground at the foot of the mountain. Now Mount Sinai was wrapped in smoke because the Lord had descended on it in fire. The smoke of it went up like the smoke of a kiln, and the whole mountain shook violently. And as the sound of the trumpet grew louder and louder . . . . the Lord came down on Mount Sinai, to the top of the mountain . . . . And God spoke . . . [in the thunder] (Ex 19:14-20:1).

The theophany from Mt. Sinai was in keeping with several other signs during this period: (a) Moses' staff, (b) the Ten Plagues, (c) the Red Sea, (d) manna and quail, (e) water from a rock, and (f) deliverance from the Amalekites (Ex 7-17), and so on. Together, these signs reinforced to his people, God's deity.

---

30   Sign ('ow*th*) has several uses in the Old Testament: as a symbol or communicative device pointing to something else, such as Cain's mark, tribal colors, and creation signs that mark the seasons, day and night, and so forth; authentication of God's presence and action (the theophany from Mt. Sinai, Ex 19) or of a prophet speaking for God; an extraordinary display of God's power, usually for salvational purposes, for example, his polemical destruction of Egyptian power when He delivered Israel (Ex 10:1-2); a sign as a sacrament, for example, the sign of circumcision and the Sabbath (Ex 31:12-17) (Mounce 2006, 42).

Second, God pronounced his divinity and lordship right at the outset of the Mosaic instructions, employing the Ten Words to teach what *God is like and not like*:

> And God spoke all these words: "I AM the LORD your GOD who brought you out of the land of Egypt, from the house of slavery. THERE ARE NO OTHER GODS BUT ME. DO NOT MAKE OR WORSHIP IMAGES [ICONS] OF ME. For I the LORD your GOD am a jealous god, visiting the sins of the fathers on the children to the third and fourth generation of those who despise me, but showing loyal love to thousands of those who love me and keep my words. DO NOT USE MY NAME, THE LORD YOUR GOD, IN VAIN, for I will not hold him guiltless. REMEMBER TO SET THE SABBATH DAY APART. Six days you shall labor, and do all your work, but the seventh day is a sabbath to the LORD your GOD." (Ex 20:1-10; cf., also 19:4-6)

Third, together with the theophany, the Ten were a *test* to see if the Israelites would trust him and simply follow instructions (much as he did with Adam and Eve).

> When the people saw the thunder and lightning and heard the trumpet and saw the mountain in smoke, they trembled with fear. They stayed at a distance and said to Moses, "Speak to us yourself and we will listen. But do not have God speak to us or we will die." Moses said to the people, "Do not be afraid. God has come to *test* you [the Ten Words plus supporting signs], so that the fear of God will be with you to keep you from sinning." (Ex 20:18-20; cf., also 15:22-16:36)

Fourth, at the same time, the Ten Words appear to be the revelatory core of the Covenant. They created a new reality, a promise of hope for what God intended for his chosen people, what they could be, what he would make of them, in the future. They appear to reflect a similar pattern as the Creation words, in which God spoke, or in this case wrote, the pertinent creative words, a kind of promise-fulfillment. Subsequently, the Ten Words were expanded into dozens of case laws that covered every aspect of life as it was then lived. "'I AM the LORD your GOD who brought you out of the land of Egypt, from the house of slavery'" (Ex 20:1); "Honor your father and your mother, so that you may live long in the land the Lord your God is giving you" (Ex 20:12); "Do not covet your neighbor's house [which they did not yet have]" (Ex 20:17); "If you carefully observe all these commands I am giving you to follow--to love the Lord your God, to walk in all his ways and to hold fast to him . . . the Lord your God, as he promised you, will put the terror and fear of you on the whole land, wherever you go" (Dt 11:22, 25); "I am making this covenant with its oath, not only with you who are standing here this day in the presence of the LORD our God, but also with those who are not here today [future generations]" (Dt 29:14-15; cf., also Ex 13:14; Dt 7:7-13; 8:18).

Fifth, the Ten Words provided the parameters for a covenant people: what they could or could not be and do, paralleling what God was like and not like:

HONOR YOUR FATHER AND MOTHER, that your days may be long in the land that the LORD your GOD is giving you. DO NOT MURDER. DO NOT FORNICATE [COMMIT ADULTERY]. DO NOT STEAL. DO NOT GIVE FALSE TESTIMONY [LIE] AGAINST YOUR NEIGHBOR. DO NOT COVET ANYTHING OF YOUR NEIGHBOR'S: his house, wife, servants, animals or anything else that is your neighbor's. (Ex 20:12-17)

And now, O Israel, what does the Lord your God ask of you but to fear the Lord your God, to walk in all his ways, to love him, to serve the Lord your God with all your heart and with all your soul, and to observe the Lord's commands and decrees that I am giving you today for your own good? (Dt 10:12-13; cf., also Lv 21:8; 19:26-37; Ex 21:1; 23:32-33; 34:10-14)

Sixth, the Ten Words explicated what "Love God only," and "Love your neighbor as yourself" involves: "Showing love to a thousand generations of those who love me" (Ex 20:6; see also 20:1-11); "Love the Lord your God with all your heart and with all your soul and with all you strength" (Dt 6:5); "love your neighbor as yourself. I am the Lord" (Ex 20:12-17; Lv 19:18). The Israelites did not have a history of treating each other with love, and had endured harsh treatment in Egypt. They needed further instruction if they were going to love God and love their neighbor.

Seventh, the Ten Words instructed them in such a way, by example and explicit instruction, so as to teach others, first their children, and eventually the nations:

> These commandments that I give you [the children of the first
> generation of covenant members] today are to be upon your hearts.
> Impress them on your children. Talk about them when you sit at
> home and when you walk along the road, when you lie down and
> when you get up. Link them to what you do and to what you
> think--your hands and your minds, and put them up on the
> doorframes of your houses and on your gates. (Dt 6:1-12, 20-25)

"Although the whole earth is mine, you will be for me a kingdom of priests and a holy nation" (Ex 19:6; see also Ex 13:9-10, 14-16; 15:1, 20-21).

Conclusions, Implications, and Recommendations

In conclusion, the Mt. Sinai-Mosaic Covenant episode is a rich case study. And as is so often the case, the real story is better than any fiction. The entire cultural scene of the renewal of the Covenant and accompanying Mosaic Instructions (Torah) focused on God conducting the renewal. Every part of the setting and actual events in the Sinai are set within God's sovereign plan and purpose conducted through his covenantal dealings with his chosen people.

The text reveals that the Israelites were in extreme distress and could not save themselves. First, God's people had to be liberated, which was followed by renewing the Covenant. Everything that happened to God's covenant people was a fulfillment of God's promise and was to their benefit. Their rescue from famine *to* Egypt, the harsh slavery they endured and their rescue *from* Egypt, the deprivations and wanderings in the wilderness, all prepared them to be revived in the covenant with their God and to be renewed as a nation.

From the stipulations and case laws we can tell that their behavior was most likely far different from that of the God with whom they were in covenant. Yes, the Israelites had generously donated to building the tabernacle and may have possessed good intentions, yet faced every deprivation and new experience with fear and unbelief. In fact, this latter deficiency prevented the generation liberated from slavery from entering the Promised Land (Heb 3:7-19).

God set his covenant renewal with the children of Israel in condescending[31] grace. He miraculously delivered them from the Egyptians and from the deprivations of the wilderness. He led them through repeated discipline, including warnings to attend and to remember. The centerpiece of the entire scene was the Ten Words of God--the creative core of a covenantal way of life. The Ten Words were accompanied by wondrous and unmistakable signs of deity-- clear indications that was God dealing directly with his people. These signs revealed what God was like and not like. They tested the people to see if they would obey--a sign of faith (they failed). They created hope of a new humanity. They set boundaries around what a covenant people was like. They explained love in action. They were taught in order to teach others: their children and outsiders.

Covenant appears to be the primary way for unrelated parties in the Ancient Near East to express long-term loyalty and relationship. Covenant

---

31 God stooped to created finite, covenantal analogies of himself (taken from Calvin's use of the term "accommodation"; Battles 1977, 19-38); see Horton 2006, 10).

pervades on several levels: the cultural way for unrelated parties to relate, cultural expressions of personal and social customs, and, possibly, an indication of the structure of, or paradigm for, reality.

The biblical text indicates that the Israelites already had a highly developed culture, with laws and other social institutions. There is also evidence of latitude for applying the actual stipulations and evidence of laws other than those recorded by Moses. The leaders, as the people's shepherds, were given these written rules to conduct themselves as covenant examples, to make good and just laws based on them, and to make good and just decisions in keeping with them. Furthermore, in order to hold them accountable, the people themselves were read the whole Mosaic Instructions once a year so that they too would remember what covenant people were to be like. Their calling as a people was to love the Lord with all their being, to love one another, and to teach these things to the next generation and to outsiders.

Some scholars conclude from this that rather than the Mosaic Instructions constituting the actual "law of the land" for the Commonwealth of Israel, the Ten Words and succeeding case laws were a body of authoritative givens: stipulations and cases for leaders to follow as they developed and enforced laws to rule the country. They represent the divine character for a specific people and period of time, and thus, can be said to be normative for all covenant peoples in all ages and cultures.

This research argues that the Ten Words were the centerpiece of the Mosaic Instructions, something like the instructional stipulations of the Mosaic Covenant. They provided the parameters and criteria for what the covenantal way of life entailed and what it did not, and paralleled the character of God himself.

History reveals that while some Israelites (the "remnant") grasped the essentials of the Covenant and passed on this faith to others from generation to generation, the vast majority practiced a kind of dead-end "designer religion." This majority enjoyed selective benefits of the Covenant, all the while dabbling in the cultural and religious ways of life of every other society with whom they came into contact. What is remarkable is that despite the long history of rampant disobedience and placing their faith in everything other than God, the covenantal way of life has been preserved and is still practiced today.

Today, over one billion people look to the Mosaic Covenant as their founding event. It continues to be annually memorialized in the *Pascha* Feast by the Jewish people, and recited in Christian catechisms 3400 years later. New believers are still being inducted and discipled to become functioning members of the covenant community.

CHAPTER 5

CASE TWO: PAUL TO THE EPHESIANS:
THE TEN WORDS IN THE NEW TESTAMENT

Introduction

Around 62 A.D., a letter was received in the Province of Asia from the Imperial Capitol at Rome that would prove to be one of the most influential in history. This is a case study of that letter, its intended audience, its author, and above all, its meaning and significance.

Critical scholars have raised questions regarding both the author and the audience. Most recent scholarship concludes that there is stronger evidence to support Paul's authorship of the Epistle to the Ephesians than precisely to which church it was written (Barth 1974, 41). [32] Despite the skepticism of some scholars of both its historicity and relevance, this letter provides a very intimate understanding of the worldviews of early Christians in the Roman Province of Asia, as well as what the community of the covenant entails for new believers of all generations.

This study provides a thick description of the real-world setting of the lives and cultures of the author and his intended audience. It explicitly retells their story at the time the letter was received, emphasizing the meaning of Paul's communication to them. Following this introduction of the particular case, the multi-layered fabric of the background context is described in detail, followed by the summary of the text and the immediate setting for the letter. The findings are then analyzed, including how the Ten Words were employed in instructing the

---

32 "All witnesses except those mentioned [P46, ℵ, B, 424c, 1739, plus Basil, Origen, Tertullian, and Ephraem] include the words ἐν Ἐφέσω (*en Efeso*), the Committee decided to retain them, but enclosed within square brackets" (Metzger 2000, 532). It could be a circular letter to the Province of Asia, similar to Colossians.

Ephesians, or believers of Asia, how to live as covenantal believers. Finally, conclusions, implications, and recommendations are proffered.

Case. Paul's Epistle to the Ephesians and his use of the Ten Words to introduce his audience to covenant living.

Research question (RQ). By what means and to what extent were the Ten Words (Commandments) used to disciple the Ephesians into the covenantal way of life, or to become functioning members of the covenant community? Subsidiary Questions: (1) What/who is the focus of this case or cultural scene? (2) What does the text itself report about the Ephesian (Gentile) former way of life (worldview), and why the Ephesians needed Paul's instruction? (3) What does the New Covenant entail, of what does the covenantal way of life consist, and how is this new way different from their former way of life? (4) By what means are the Ten Words used to instruct the Ephesians? And (5) To what extent was the Covenant or the Ten Words used to instruct the Ephesians and in what ways are they instruments of grace?

Sources. The biblical text is a rich transcription of several overlapping sources: Luke, the "participant observer" and official news source of the Pauline party (The Acts of the Apostles); the primary human "protagonist," Paul the Apostle, who introduced the early Ephesians/Asians to Christ (The Epistle of Paul to the Ephesians); Timothy, the main pastor assigned to the Roman Province of Asia at the time, received Paul's pastoral correspondence during his tenure (The First and Second Letters of Paul to Timothy); and a later primary interlocutor of the Asian Christians, the Apostle John (The Revelation of John). Secondary literature is consulted as well.[33]

---

[33] This author assumes divine inspiration for the biblical text, which is the primary source for this case study, per its own self definition of inspiration (2 Pt 1:16-21). It is therefore absolutely authoritative. That said, he also recognizes that the actual population is no longer available, and that the text can be used as the transcript of the primary research conducted at the time of the event or shortly thereafter. Therefore, it is this text and not the actual episode that will be mined for clues/data, as is similarly the case in all historical research.

Fabric of the Context

The Anatolian Peninsula, comprising most of modern Turkey, lies at the intersection of Asia and Europe. One of the oldest continually inhabited regions in the world, with a long history, it became home to many Christian churches in the first century A.D. Several factors make up the cultural scene.

Multi-layered Fabric of the Background Context

Geography. The area encompassed by the Roman province of Asia stretched from the Aegean coast in the west to Philomelium (modern Aksehir, Turkey) in the east, and from the Sea of Marmara in the north to the strait between the mainland and Rhodes in the south. The province is marked by long transverse ridges, 1,000 to 7,000 feet in elevation, fanning westward towards the coast from the western end of the Taurus Mountain range, and interspersed with river plains down to the Aegean Sea. The Caieus, the Hermus, and the Meander valleys are among the most fertile in the world. Traffic since the dawn of history flowed along the great ancient roads from the Euphrates or from Syria by way of the Cilician gates above Tarsus and then down these valleys. Also, the greatest and most prosperous cities sprang up in those valleys, cities from which first Hellenism, then the Pax Romana, and finally, Christianity radiated over the whole region (Ramsay 1907, 265).

The region's climate is temperate, with hot, "malarial" summers and mild, wet winters. The interior becomes harsher the further east one goes. The province has a wealth of natural resources, including mineral deposits (iron, copper, gold, limestone, marble, pumice, clay). The hilly landscape lent itself to animal husbandry, and its dyestuffs and woolen textiles had long been famous.

History. Anatolia had a long and complex history before the Christian apostle Paul arrived in approximately A.D. 52. Certain cultural traits are definitively historically traceable: the importance of family and kinship; the town as basic social unit, of which Strabo estimated there were over 10,000 on the central plains (1903, 12 & 14), from Neolithic times polytheistic religion, almost always including one form or another of mother goddess. From the indigenous Hatti, who had an advanced early civilization, later generations of Anatolians received a written alphabet, city-planning, jewelry and pottery-making. From the long-past immigrant Hittites they received a law code, vassal treaties, and the penchant for polyculturalism, mixing traits from various cultures together in one community.

Still later, these traits were acquired by the Lydians and others, who in turn passed them on to the Greek colonists who arrived on the western coast from the twelfth century B.C. onwards. During the Panionium League of twelve Ionian cities, they learned philosophy, science and the arts, reaching its zenith in Miletus. The League was conquered in 560 by King Croessus of Lydia, then by the Persians under Darius I in 546, and then re-conquered by the Macedonians under Alexander the Great in 334-3 B.C.

Hellenism. The Greek plan to civilize the world pursued a combination of means typical of the way monism (see definitions) perpetuates itself: it conquered, established a network of Greek city-states (*poli*) either by refurbishing older cities in the Greek manner or by establishing new ones, and connected them by refurbished trade routes. Greek institutions such as the Greek language, citizen rule, the *paideia* to educate the rising generation in the Greek mold, the theater, and trade and craft guilds stamped the Greek character wherever they went. Onto this cohesive base, then, the Greeks began to synthesize strengths received from the earlier cultural influences.

The conscious aim of the poli, or city-states, founded or remade in the Greek image, was the Hellenization of the entire region. These cities established a colonial trade relationship with the surrounding countryside, which supplied the raw material for city-based industry and commerce. Their example influenced neighboring cities. The Seleucids found the Jews trusty colonists for their scheme, including, for example, the Jews of Tarsus, Antioch in Psidia, and Ephesus (Acts 13:14 ff.; 18:19-20).

With the Greek cities came the Greek Pantheon, but wherever any detailed information concerning a cult is uncovered, under a Greek (or Roman) disguise one can recognize the essential features of the old Anatolian god. Much of inner Asia Minor must have been governed originally on a theocratic system. In sharp contrast to the oriental absolutism of the native system, the secular and more democratic Greek city-state gradually encroached on the territory and privileges of the ancient temple (Ramsay 1904, 96).

Pax Romana. The Hellenistic Age was still in effect when Paul arrived in the province. The long, orderly, peaceful reign of Augustus brought stability and affluence to the empire (Dudley 1993, 124). From Augustus onwards (27 B.C. to 297 A.D.), Asia was governed by a proconsul of consular rank. It was divided into districts, which the governor or his three assistants (*legati*) visited to dispense justice. Under this administration, peace and prosperity returned to the new Roman province of Asia, although, as the province with the most resources, it was commercially exploited and heavily taxed.

"Already heavily Hellenized in the Greek custom, with Persian artistic influence, Roman civilization in the East thrived and culminated in Asia" (United Nations of Roma Vietrix, Asia Minor). In the earlier centuries of the Roman Empire the major city-states and towns were thoroughly cosmopolitan: part Greek, part Asiatic. They enjoyed a liberal measure of self-government. "Magistracies were elective; wealthy men in the same city vied with each other, and city vied with city, erecting magnificent public building projects" (Ramsay 1904, 96), founding schools and promoting education, throughout the province.

The provincial assembly, called the *koinon* of Asia, with representatives from all the major cities, met annually, rotating between the temples of the principal cities, chose *Asiarchs* (officials), passed resolutions, made appeals, sent deputations on provincial matters, and sponsored the Asian games (Ramsay 1904, 96).

Under the Roman Empire, a gradual evolution in the organization of the Greek cities toward the Roman municipal type can be traced. One of the main factors in this process was the foundation of Roman garrisons of veterans, stationed there to maintain order, such as in Antioch and Lystra in New Testament times. In the first century, Latin was the official language in the colonies. However, it never ousted Greek in general usage, and Greek soon replaced it in official documents. Education was at its highest level in the Greek cities and in the Roman colonies, and it was primarily to these that Paul went with the gospel (Ramsay 1904, 96).

Ephesus, the provincial capital, was said to have been founded in the eleventh century B.C. by Androcles of Athens. In the first century A.D. it grew to become the third cultural center of the empire, after Rome and Alexandria, with a population of around 200,000 (Trebilco 1994, 307). It was also the major port for trade with the East, connected by the Royal Road to Susa, the Persian capital. Though unimportant politically, Ephesus was noted for its extensive commerce, which supported a rich and varied culture.

After Alexander, the cultural synthesis began showing signs of disintegration due to inherent weaknesses and the political rivalries after his death. Later, the Imperial peace of Augustus began to disintegrate with the four succeeding emperors, alternating between increasing violence (Tiberius, 14-37 A.D.; Caligula, 37-41; and Nero, 54-68) interspersed with stability and progress (Claudius, 41-54) (Dudley 1993, 160-66). Nero's reign was especially hard for Jews and Christians near the Imperial center.

Culture. Due to the long and rich history of many different cultures, including native Anatolian, Western Semitic, Persian, Asian from the eastern steppes, Celt, Greek, and now Roman, the culture of the Province of Asia was a grand mixture of living, trading, intermarrying, and conquering. The population was composed of many overlying strata of races, which tended in part to lose their individuality and sink into the original Anatolian type (Orr 1915, "Asia Minor"). Generally speaking, it is possible to discern two main coexistent social systems. One may be designated the native system, predominately in the countryside and older towns, and the other the hellenistic system, in the large and newer cities (Strabo 1903).

Three basic assumptions defined the cultural milieu of the Greco-Roman world: kinship, patronage, and honor/shame (deSilva 2000). Kinship or the *familia* (Latin term for which there is no exact English equivalent) was perhaps the main pillar of society in the Province of Asia. The traditional Roman familia consisted both of blood relatives and all those attached to the household, both slaves and freed persons. The typical *domus* (house), in which the privileged few lived, is most likely the type of household-compound that hosted early churches: Cornelius's (Acts 10); possibly Mary's (Acts 12); Lydia's (Acts 16), Nympha's (Col 4:7), and Philemon's (Phlm 1:2) (Fee 2002, 5).

The *paterfamilias* was the master of his household. Under the ancient Roman law of the *gens*,[34] his rule was absolute, in the sense that no one else in the household had legal means to redress any grievances. Men married at thirty, while the average age for wives was less than eighteen. The woman thus entered the household as a teenager, whom the man had then to educate in the ways of his household. The main purpose for marriage was not love in the modern sense, and the idea that men and women might be equal partners was almost non-existent.[35] The main function of the wife was to bear legitimate children to keep the family line going. Failure to bear children, especially sons, was often a cause for divorce. Rarely did the wife join her husband and his friends at meals; if she did, she did not recline at table (as did the courtesans), but sat on a bench at

---

34 Gaius (3.17) wrote of the relationship through the male line (*agnatio*), and the unlimited power [authority] of the *paterfamilias* (Carcopino 1992, 76).

35 Aquila and Priscilla (Acts) appear to be notable exceptions (see Fee 2002 , 6).

the end. She was expected to leave after eating, when the conversation took a more public turn. According to Demosthenes, most men visited prostitutes or kept a mistress (Carcopino 1992, 92). The few promiscuous wives had to be more discreet because such an act would be considered infidelity, a matter of shame.

Slaves, of course, did all the work, both menial and clerical, including the tutoring of the children. Slavery was based initially on conquest in war, and eventually on economic need. By the late Republic, the entire economy depended upon slavery (see figure 5). Slaves had absolutely no rights before the law, evidenced by the fact that they could not even marry.

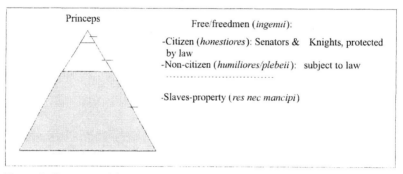

Figure 5. Roman social structure, First century A.D.

Patronage refers to the mutual relationship that existed between unequals in which each was understood to benefit the other. The Greco-Roman worldview was predicated on the reality of a world that was bottom-heavy; that is, the top few percent were the elite or privileged, and the vast majority were totally dependent on being in good standing with a patron. The paterfamilias was also the *patronus*, and every patron was also a client of his patron. "The patronus . . . was honor bound to welcome his client at his house, invite him from time to time to his table, to come to his assistance, and to make him gifts" (Carcopino 1992, 171). The poet Martial (1.49.35-6) said the patronus's importance depended on the size of his clientèle. Normally, clients were seen in the early morning in the home's *theatrium* before the business day began. Seneca, in fact, remarked that the giving and receiving of favors was the "practice that constitutes the chief bond of human society." The householder (paterfamilias) and a few higher-level slaves had the only public roles. Men were out and about most of the time.

Honor and shame ruled everything. Honor, or its opposite, disgrace, was regularly the basis for most moral appeals. A convention of what was honorable or shameful was the fabric that held Greco-Roman culture together.

A society based on the pursuit of honour, whether Homeric *kleos* or Roman *gloria*, is bound to be competitive. The man of honour is anxious to promote his own honour at the expense of the honour of others. There is only a limited amount of honour at hand, and one resents and envies the possession of it by other people. (Walcot 1973, 117; see also Wiseman 1985, 6)

Economy. In the empire everything from the entire known world flowed to the center at Rome.

The tiles and bricks, wines and fruits of Italy; the corn of Egypt and Africa; the oil of Spain; the venison, the timbers, and the wool of Gaul; the cured meats of Baetica; the dates of the oases; the marbles of Tuscany, of Greece and of Numidia; the porphyries of the Arabian Desert; the lead, silver, and copper of the Iberian Peninsula; the ivory of the Syrtes and the Mauretanias, the gold of Dalmatia and of Dacia; the tin of the Cassiterides . . . the amber of the Baltic; the papyri of the valley of the Nile; the glass of Phoenicia and of Syria; the stuffs of the Orient; the incense of Arabia; the spices, the corals, and the gems of India; the silks of the Far East. (Loane 1983, 11-59)

Carcopino wrote of the human capital to support the Empire:

> Distant subject peoples and those still more distant with whom
> they traded both within and without the imperial frontiers
> exhausted or enriched themselves to provide the city with what she
> demanded from every corner of the earth. (Carcopino 1992, 178)

There were more than one hundred fifty commercial corporations centered in
Rome to handle this gigantic commercial tide. Trade guilds began at dawn
(Carcopino 1992, 171).

Dress. Men and women, both Greek and Roman, wore similar style
clothing except for the outer garments and embellishments. Men wore the round
toga, while Greek men and women wore the rectilinear *himation*. Hairdressers'
shops (*tonsori*) for men became a kind of social club (Carcopino 1992, 157-8),
while women were usually treated at home by their slave girl.

Education. According to Tacitus, upper class newborns were often given
educated Greek nurses so that the first words they heard were proper Greek
(Carcopino 1992, 104). Quintilian (I.1.4) reported: "The alphabet and simple
reading were usually learned at home" (Carcopino 1992, 104). Next, according to
Quintilian (I.1.8), came the paedagogus, a slave who served as tutor, guardian,
and servant of the child put in his care (Carcopino 1992, 104). Schools, taught by
a magister, covered reading, writing and arithmetic, but were notoriously lax
(Carcopino 1992, 106). The final stage was grammar in Greek and Latin, and
rhetoric almost exclusively in Greek because the Romans could not allow their
sons to be less cultivated than their conquered subjects (Carcopino 1992, 108).
"The most important consequence of this was that eloquence, the end and aim
both of grammar and rhetoric, was emptied of all real content" (Carcopino 1992,
109). The sole focus of study was the classics (Carcopino 1992, 112). The liberal
arts (Roman) were only touched upon as they were mentioned in the orations
(Carcopino 1992, 120). The result of mere memorization, day after day, of

ancient texts with little relevance or even understanding, made it into pedantry, resulting in boredom and reaction against culture (Carcopino 1992, 120-121).

By the early empire, the social glue provided by the centuries old institution of the family was beginning to break down. The absolute authority of the father was eroding, resulting over time in indulgence, flagrant disobedience, and the rise of generations of idlers, described by Pliny the Younger as "the eternal spoiled child of society, who has grown accustomed to luxury and lost all sense of discipline" (Carcopino 1992, 78-9).

Over time, marriages began to be viewed more as a partnership (at least among the upper classes), entered into as a reciprocal arrangement between two young people with the consent of their fathers and a few friends as witnesses. B y the end of the first century many Roman marriages were childless (Carcopino 1992, 90). Instead of spending most of their time indoors, wealthier women would visit friends, go for walks. Women even began to compete with men in business, the arts, sports, literature discussions, politics and law, and so on (Carcopino 1992, 91).

The practice of patronage deteriorated as well. Standards of decency and order changed with the inroads of new customs and the general breakdown of order. This social disintegration was only faintly reflected in the masses of non-citizens, so far as they worked in the households of the wealthy.

Public entertainment. The absorbing occupation and distraction of cultivated Romans was giving and hearing recitations, whether in the home auditoria of the wealthy or "declaiming" at some important event (Carcopino 1992, 193, 195). Striving for eloquence gave way to eloquence for its own sake, and content diminished, resulting in what Caligula described as "sand without mortar" (Carcopino 1992, 200).

Greek culture gave way to the silver age of Latin literature: Tacitus, Juvenal, Lucan, Petronius, Seneca, Martial, Italicus, Flaccus, Pliny, Quintilian (Dudley 1993, 222). By the first century A.D., however, the theater was giving way to an even bigger stage, the amphitheater, with violent and incestuous productions brutalizing the senses and arousing the passions of the mob (Carcopino 1992, 223). These spectacles were reproduced on a lesser scale in provincial capitals. The Greek games, by contrast, were colorless and decreasingly popular, even though competed in the nude--a shock to Latin sensibilities (Carcopino 1992, 245).

At the time of Claudius, the Roman calendar contained 159 holidays, not including local fests, of which ninety-three were devoted to games given at public expense (Carcopino 1992, 204-5). Although every holiday had its religious, if distant, significance, the state-sponsored games, such as the gladiatorial contests, became completely secularized for political ends.

The typical Roman day wound down in the afternoon to the baths. Sports in the Greek style, then to the *sudatoria* to continue the sweat, to the *caldarum*, to equalize the body heat with the ambient temperature, and then a quick dive in the *frigidarium* to cool down. Men's and women's bath times were separated by law. This was followed by a late dinner, with many courses enjoyed to the full, complete with belching, spitting, course jokes, and the like (Carcopino 1992, 270-72).

Philosophy. The predominate philosophy of the day was Stoicism (as modified by Panaetius and Posidonius): harmony that pervades the cosmos, beneficent providence, innateness of nature, possibility of progress towards virtue due to man's spark of divinity that will return him to his origin at death, and a tendency to extreme republicanism. However, it is safe to say that the belief system was in reality Stoicism mixed with astrology, since many were also members of some mystery cult or brotherhood.

Religion. In the early empire, religion was practiced on at least three levels simultaneously: (1) one's family religion, (2) the state religion, always with religious overtones, but principally an increasingly secular worship of the emperor by the first century, and (3) the religion of personal choice, one or more of the thousands of mystery cults.

Family religion from ancient times was centered around the hearth gods and on a polytheism of place, a kind of animism, in which every stone, forest, spring, mountain, glade, crossroads, and so on, had its spirit and its local rituals (Jones and Pennick 1999, 25-58). Usually, but not always, the paterfamilias required the household to serve his gods, since the gods were looked upon as responsible for "order," for causing and maintaining things the way they are (Fee 2002, 6).

State religion. Each city-state elevated a devolved deity or deities with their accompanying cult (rituals, temples, and *sacerdotes*) to be acknowledged by the populace as a whole. The state religion for Anatolians usually centered on some form of earth-mother and her consorts of fecundity. Greeks had their Olympic pantheon of anthropomorphic deities, and Romans their adapted deities. Because the state cult "plumbed" ancient superstitions (Carcopino 1992, 131), families could follow without qualm the cultural religion in addition to their own private rites.

Many cities of Asia recognized each other's cults and festivals, commemorated by striking "alliance-coins" on which the patron deities of the two cities are represented side by side. In A.D. 56, devotees claimed Artemis (Diana) of Ephesus as the goddess "whom all Asia and the civilized world worships" (Ramsay 1904), because Ephesus concluded more alliances of this kind than any other city of Asia.

Ephesus owed its chief renown to its temple of Artemis, one of the seven wonders of the ancient world. "For over a thousand years this goddess with her temple provided a focal point for the colorful religious, economic, and cultural life of her worshippers" (Krystek 1998). Built east of the city on the river Cayster overlooking the bay, it was four times the size of the Parthenon in Athens--400 X 200 feet, with 128 pillars sixty feet high (Nelson 1986, 345-6; see also Blake and

Edmonds, 119). Its grounds were a place of asylum, and on feast days over one million would watch the procession.

During the imperial period, state religion became the divinization of the emperor. Augustus had seemed a saviour to the Asian peoples; they deified him as the saviour of mankind, and worshiped him with the most wholehearted devotion as the God incarnate in human form (Ramsay 1904). In the Greco-Roman cities of the province, however, "Romans had the feeling not of following a liturgy but of complying with a rule of etiquette" (Carcopino 1992, 208). Thus, the emperor cult actually accelerated secularization. This was more true of the educated classes, whereas the multitudes were increasingly entertained by the state subsidized festivals of the gods (Carcopino 1992, 122).

Personal-mystical. Religion during the Empire was characterized by two phenomena: personal religion and syncretism. For the first time in history, religion became a matter of personal choice. Thousands of cults flooded in from the East and "flourished in an easy and tolerant polytheism" (Dudley 1993, 229), with "more affinity and mutual understanding between these diverse religions than rivalry" (Carcopino 1992, 130). Brotherhoods filled the gaps of village life left behind and the depersonalization of city life.

Mithraism, spread chiefly through the military, was probably the most widespread in Paul's day (Dudley 1993, 230). Other popular cults included (a) Cybele and Attis, (b) Baalim, (c) Dea Syra, (e) Isis and Serapis, and (f) Bel and Palmyra. Whatever their origin, these cults shared many common features: (a) mediation of the cult by sacred priests to profane constituents, (b) doctrine based on revelation, (c) preliminary initiation rite, (d) periodic asceticism, (e) astrological speculations and divination, and (f) message of hope (Cumont 1911, 181-194; see also Levi 1936).

At the same time, local divinities were absorbed, Hellenized, and then Romanized. Through the common process (synthesis) of Hellenization, oriental revelation and Greek philosophy interpenetrated one another and fused into one.

This transformation, together with astrology, resulted in ease of converting Romans to the gods of the East (Carcopino 1992, 128-29).

Christianity. The quickly shifting religious atmosphere set the stage for Christianity. Superficially, it was similar to the other religions, yet most scholars concur that Christianity towered above them (see Loisy 1922, 363).

> Christianity appears as the last and greatest of the universal
> religions. Like its predecessors [oriental mystery religions], it
> offered through ritual and sacrament a personal spiritual
> experience, and proclaimed life after death and redemption through
> a divine savior. Such ideas were already familiar in the Greco-
> Roman world. (Dudley 1993, 232)

The findings will demonstrate whether or not their assessment is justified. Christianity also spread in its early stages with ease due to the *Koine* (trade language) (Fee 2002).

Summary of the Text

According to available records, Paul the Apostle was the first to bring the "mystery of Christ"[36] to the province of Asia. On a layover while traveling by sea from Corinth, in Achaeia (Greece), to Cesarea, in Syria, in perhaps A.D. 51, Paul engaged the Jews in an already-existing synagogue at Ephesus, the capital city, on the subject of the Kingdom of God. He left the mature Christian couple, Priscilla and Aquila, to continue the contact. Natives of Pontus, they had recently been exiled from Rome by Claudius in A.D. 49 (Acts 18:2; see also Seutonius 1883, 25.4).

Upon his return overland the following year, Paul found twelve disciples who had evidently come to faith through the exhortation of Apollos, a Christian

---

36 A biblical "mystery," in contradistinction to how Greeks used this term, is something/someone previously unrevealed but now, in God's time, clearly revealed (Eph 3:2-6). For the Greeks, *musterion* was something hidden, secret, a secret teaching, religious ceremony/rite or doctrine; that which is known only to the *myustes,* the initiated; in *Aesychlus, Herodotus* onward (*BDAG,* 3d ed. 661-2; *Abbott-Smith* 1960, 298).

teacher from Alexandria who had passed through on the way to Greece. Their "Pentecost" experience when Paul baptized them launched Paul's three year ministry in Ephesus. Paul was seemingly able to pick up at the synagogue where he left off. He taught boldly for three months until the extreme obstinacy of some Jews prompted him to move his teaching to a neutral hall, that of Tyrannus. Paul also made sure, through his own enterprise, that the new believers were not responsible for his or his team's living expenses.

He continued lecturing publicly and teaching "from house to house . . . . so that all the Jews and Greeks who lived in the province of Asia heard the Word of the Lord" (Acts 19:8-10; 20:20-21). This may have included upwards of forty cities and larger towns in the province. The text records what occurred next.

> God did extraordinary miracles through Paul, [and] when this
> became known to the Jews and Greeks living in Ephesus they were
> all seized with the fear of the Lord, and the name of the Lord Jesus
> was held in high honor (Acts 19:11, 17).

> Many of those who believed now came and openly confessed their
> evil deeds. A number who had practiced sorcery brought their
> scrolls together and burned them publicly [and] the value of the
> scrolls came to [over $2 million]. In this way the Word of the Lord
> spread widely and grew in power (Acts 19:18-20).

This kind of real change could not help but provoke "no little commotion"[37] (Acts 19:23) with the opposing spiritual power center. The immense power of the temple of Artemis, entrenched for centuries, included the actual temple activity and power structure, the prosperous guild that made shrines for tourists, other adjacent businesses such as hostelries, the general populace's pride, and actual customs and laws. Demetrius plumbed all that power and emotion when he incited the silversmiths to riot against the rapidly growing Christian movement.

---

37 *Litotes,* a figure of speech common in Greek literature and especially in Acts (cf. 12:18; 21:39): emphasizes something by stressing its opposite (Wason 2006, 4).

83

Quickly, a huge mob rushed down Harbor Street and filled the theater (capacity 25,000 people), shouting for several hours: "Great is Artemis of the Ephesians; Great is Artemis of the Ephesians!" (Acts 19:28, 34).[38] It took some deft leadership on the part of the city clerk to calm the crowd and persuade them to disperse.

When the uproar subsided, Paul bade farewell to the disciples, and left for Macedonia. After perhaps half a year visiting churches and encouraging the disciples throughout Greece, he called an emotional meeting with the elders from Ephesus (and perhaps the province) (Acts 20:13-38). Because of his desire to be in Jerusalem by Pentecost, this meeting was actually held at Miletus, southwest from Ephesus on the coast. Their mutual love was evident as he taught and encouraged them one final time. Throughout his association with them, Paul's guiding biblical principle had been the words of Jesus: "It is more blessed to give than to receive" (Acts 20:35-21:1).

The new believers of Ephesus and the province continued to receive much apostolic attention throughout the New Testament period. Timothy was assigned as their pastor for at least a decade. Tychicus also paid a pastoral visit, bringing the instructional Epistle of Paul to the Ephesians. And, more than a decade later, John, one of the original disciples, was directed by the "Son of Man, standing among the seven golden lampstands" to write an exhortative letter to "the angel of the church in Ephesus," acknowledging their perseverance, but exhorting them to consider what was their greatest love (Rev 1:13; 2:1).

Immediate Setting

The setting for this case study concerns the human author of the letter, the audience, and the God who authored the whole situation. God is the main focus in this case study, and so is dealt with first. In the Old Testament case of the

---

38 One can find, going in the direction of the theater, a stall for the silversmith guild near the market (Ramsay 1904, 224). Also, several public halls, such as that of Tyrannus have been located (Harland, 2003, 6).

84

children of Israel in Sinai, a dramatic theophany [39] preceded both his deliverance of them from slavery in Egypt and his giving them the Mosaic Instructions on Mt. Sinai. In the New Testament case of the new Ephesian believers, Paul's covenantal understanding prompted him to precede his instructions to them with an exaltation of praise. He began the letter by proclaiming the incomparable power of God (Eph 1:18-23), his immeasurable love (Eph 3:14-21), and his guaranteed great salvation in Christ (Eph 1:3-14; 3:1-13). Therefore, Paul could exhort them to live their new life in a manner worthy of God and his magnificent calling.

Second, Paul wrote to the church(es) in Ephesus, the capital city of the Province of Asia, most probably as representative of all the churches of the province, from the Mamertine Prison under the very windows of Nero's palace in Rome in the early 60s. [40] Also, because of his own present bondage on their behalf, Paul could exhort them to live their new life in a manner worthy of their calling as covenant people (Eph 3:1; 4:1; Col 1:24).

At the same time, Paul was also Christ's apostle. Just as God chose Israel not because of any merit (Dt 7) but solely due to his free grace, in like manner Paul was chosen and made an apostle solely due to God's grace. On this basis, he wrote to the Ephesians/believers in Asia under the authority granted him by the king of the universe, as his apostle, his messenger, just as Moses was appointed God's prophet and leader one and a half millennia prior.

Specifically, Paul was the apostle to the Gentiles. The distinct ethnic group Moses had constituted as the prototype covenant people of God had come to reduce the Covenant to be a privilege only for insiders. Paul's specific charge

---

39 Physical manifestation of divine presence (Currid 2001).

40 A real imprisonment in Rome toward the end of Paul's life, assumed by most conservative scholars, yields this date. "Those who reject Pauline authorship usually date Ephesians in the period 70-90 . . . . It cannot be much later than about 90, for it seems to be referred to by Clement of Rome, who is usually thought to have written his letter ca. A.D. 96" (Carson, Moo, and Morris 1992, 309).

was to extend the Covenant to include the Gentiles, people from every people group on earth. Now, the Ephesians and others who formerly were excluded from the Covenant would be included and would inherit all the privileges thereof. And, instead of being co-terminous with real geography, the covenant community would now encompass God's people living wherever they were, dispersed throughout the nations.

Third, two realities of his audience in Ephesus/Asia bear on what Paul wrote to them: their former worldview and their new "calling" in Christ. First, Paul couched his instructions in four key words counter to their *former* worldview: (1) *humility* (lower one's self-estimation); (2) *gentleness* (not being overly self-impressed); (3) *patience* (slow to anger); (4) *bearing* with each other in love (Eph 4:1-2). Paul was aware that he was writing to a mixed audience, both to those who had previously oppressed some who were now "fellow citizens," or had at least dismissed them as having little value, and to some who had previously envied and hated those in whose homes they now worshiped. Most of his audience, even those who had very little, would be caught up in the values of the empire: cutthroat competition and grasping for more money, influence, and power. Paul boldly communicated that the values of Christ's kingdom are opposite those of the empire. Whether they had lost prestige and status involuntarily or currently enjoyed these privileges, he urged them to rejoice and to refuse to let these values rule or characterize them. Because of their position in Christ, they could bear with each other's differences in love.

Furthermore, Paul couched his instructions (Heb *torah*; Grk *didaskalia*) in terms of his audience's most important, and new, reality, their "calling" (4:1), how they "learned Christ" (4:20). They "were taught already to put off the old self, which is being corrupted [corroded] by its deceitful desires, in order to be made new . . . and to put on the new self, created to be like God in true righteousness and holiness" (4:22-24). Paul described their present newness of life (Eph 2:1-22) as analogous to the position of the Israelites when recently released from slavery in Egypt (Ex 6-18). Just as God personally delivered the children of Israel in a mighty way from Egypt before renewing the Covenant with them, so too Paul was communicating to the new believers in Asia that they had also been mightily and completely delivered from their "former way of life," from enslavement to sin and their worldview's sinful customs, in order to be united in new covenant with God in Christ. For this final reason, because they had been made new, Paul's astute instructions were valid for their consideration.

Findings

The findings are taken primarily from Paul's letter of instruction to the believers in Asia, the Epistle to the Ephesians. In a profound manner he exemplifies the New Testament "use" of the Law (Instructions). [41] Following Moses' lead, Paul repeated the Ten Words for new believers, members of the community of the Covenant, set in a paean of God's incomparable greatness in Christ. In so doing, he indirectly applied the instructions to their Hellenistic worldview.

Apparently, one of the main purposes of the Ten Words for Moses and for Paul was to teach people new to the Covenant how to shift their paradigm for living from their pagan worldview perspective to covenantal thinking. Paul's instructions to the new believing communities in the Roman Province of Asia parallel the Mosaic lead in purpose, number, content, and (covenantal) instructional tone (figure 6 below). Both historical examples are meant to describe the "calling" or "new way of life," as opposed to the old, for new believers, new citizens of the covenant community.

---

[41] Note: Paul did not concentrate on exegesis of Old Testament texts (the Ten Words) in his communication to the Ephesians, but on hermeneutics: how to apply the Ten Words to their situation. He had already done the exegesis.

OLD TESTAMENT	NEW TESTAMENT
1. Theonomic vision of God (Ex 3-4; 19)	1. Incomparable greatness of God in Christ (Eph 1; 3)
2. Rescue Israelites from slavery in Egypt (Ex 4-17)	2. Once excluded from Christ, now included in the Covenant in Christ (Eph 2)
3. Renew the Covenant (Ex 19:3-8, 24; 24:3-11)	3. Calling in Christ (Eph 4:1; 5:30); put off old/put on new (4:22-24)
4. Mosaic (10) Instructions for new Covenant members (Ex 20)	4. Pauline (10) Instructions for new New Covenant members (Eph 4-6)

Figure 6. Case studies compared

As the Ten Words were readily remembered anchor points of the Mosaic Covenant for the Children of Israel over a millennium prior, they continue as memorable anchor points for Paul's covenantal thinking (Hoffecker, Class Notes, March 2008).[42] In order to locate Paul's usage and expression of his covenantal understanding of the Ten Words, standard historical-grammatical exegetical principles need to be observed. The grammatical context has priority for guiding understanding, then the historical context, including salvation/revelation history. Third, one should not expect necessarily a word-for-word restatement of the Ten Words.

Prior to examining the grammatical contexts, the differing historical contexts for Moses and Paul need to be understood. Moses lived in a Semitic, Hebrew context, Paul in a Eurasian, Hellenistic-Roman *sitz im leben*. Paul's was fifteen hundred or so years and multiple civilizations later, from late Bronze to

---

42 All the instructions (commands) in Ephesians 4-5 can be taken today as expansions of the Mosaic instructions one and two, or are the positive sides or new implications of the prohibitive commands, in keeping with the rubric of "having put off the old," "put on the new," and possibly justifying the tradition of deducing positive implications of the original Ten Words cast in the negative.

late Hellenistic-early Roman Empire. A basically nomadic-pastoral people who had recently been enslaved and forced to work in cities was Moses' context, versus urban-dwellers for centuries in Paul's.

Reality for both was sacramental and mediated, although the expressions were quite different. The religious surroundings of the Hebrews was a kind of henotheism. The standard magical-sacramental view of reality mediated by priests had a slightly different cast of characters and conventions tied to local geography and agriculture in each case, whether Canaanite, Mesopotamian, or Egyptian. On the other hand, the Ephesians were polycultural, polyreligious, yet driven by the hellenistic propensity to synthesize hylomorphically (one Ideal stamped into all similar forms, and dissenting details eliminated), and to yield to the overriding determinism of fate. Yet, the common denominator of all their religious choices was also a complicated magico-sacramental view of reality that needed to be mediated by priest or philosopher. Whereas for the neighbors of the Israelites, only the king or priest was in some way titanic (divine soul in human form), for the Ephesians, theoretically all men were titanic and so could become one with the divine, if only the proper formula were discovered and followed.

When one examines closely the grammatical contexts of the Ten Words in Exodus and in Ephesians, it is helpful to ask the question: what issue is being addressed by each of the Ten Words? In the literature there is very little exploration of this level of exegesis, much less agreement. It is this author's studied contention that the issue in the Exodus account for the so-called first table, particularly the first Word, was one of lordship and ultimate allegiance. To Israel God said that he alone rescued them from the false incarnation of divine power in Egypt, just as he alone created and providentially governs all nature; they had only him and no other to thank. The issue could be summarized: due lordship, allegiance-relationship and consequent gratitude.

The Ephesians, on the other hand, were accustomed to personal choice in questions of ultimate spiritual allegiance. However, a Christian church is not made up of followers of many gods, nor is ultimate lordship a product of integrative/ synthetic processes. Paul wrote that there is one body, one Spirit, one hope, one Lord, one faith, one baptism, one God and Father of all who is over all, through all, and in all (Eph 4:4-6). Same issue, different context. One thing we know, their context cannot be conflated historically with the ecumenical context of today.

Likewise, this author's study finds that the second Word deals with the related issue of where the line is drawn between divinity and the created and how distinctly it is drawn. Both contexts blur the lines, and they both involve deity within reality, as we know it, and at least some men in divinity. God says to leave the line distinct and where he made it, between himself and all else. For the Israelites, surrounded by gods and their icons, he commanded that they not make icons of him or worship anything else as god. Rather, they were to rely on God alone. For the Ephesians, whose polytheism was being assimilated by neo-Stoicism, their primary problem of faulty thinking drove how they worshiped. Paul did not say to not make icons or idols. Instead, he told them that their thinking needed to be reconstructed.

The third Word is also related. Hellenistic Ephesians continued an assumption also true of the Mesopotamians and Egyptians of attributing all power to their god or human incarnation. They would even wield his name in their competitive relations with one another, imprecating in the name of their god or swearing by his name to achieve some benefit, possibly in faint memory of God's creative Word. This practice is akin to Constantine (and others) waging war under the sign of the cross. To the Israelites, God said that he alone is ultimate power, and he is not at human beck and call; his words alone are creative and can cause things to happen. They were not to swear by his or any other divine name. Almost certainly, Moses was not speaking simply of the penchant for cursing. In the New Testament, James wrote that our tongue incites much evil, not in a magical way, but for actual hearers. Perhaps, it is in this vein that Paul wrote to the Ephesians that such talk corrupts the speaker and has no magical power over situations or people. For this reason, he instructed them to only use words that are good for building up, fitting, giving grace to hearers. Paul also exhorted them to not grieve the Holy Spirit by assuming we humans have magical power, including our words (4:29-30;5:4).

MOSAIC TEN WORDS (Ex 20; Dt 5)	PAULINE TEN WORDS (Eph 4-6)
1. I am the Lord your God, who brought you out of the land of Egypt, out of the house of slavery. You shall have no other gods beside me (Ex 20:2-3)	1. There is one body, one Spirit, one hope, one Lord, one faith, one baptism, one God and Father of all who is over all, through all, and in all (Eph 4:4-6)
2. You shall not make an image of any other created thing, nor bow down to them or serve them for I am a jealous God visiting iniquity on those who hate me and steadfastly loving those who love me and keep my commandments (20:4-6)	2. No longer live as the Gentiles in the futility of their thinking, having their understanding blinded and alienated from the life of God because of the ignorance in them due to their hardened hearts (4:17-19)
3. Do not vainly use the Lord's name (20:11)	3. Let no corrupting talk out of your mouths (4:29-30; 5:4)
4. Remember the Sabbath day to keep it holy (20:8-11)	4. Be thankful, sing and make music to the Lord from the heart. . . . Look carefully how you walk, not as unwise, making the most of the time for the days are evil (5:4, 15-20)
5. Honor your father and mother (20:12)	5. Let all bitterness, wrath, anger, clamor, slander, and malice be put away; obey them; submit to one another in reverence to Christ (4:31; 5:21; 6:1-8).
6. Do not murder (20:13)	6. Do not sin in your anger; don't let the sun go down on your anger (4:26)
7. Do not commit adultery (20:14)	7. Sexual immorality and all impurity must not even be hinted at among you (5:3)
8. Do not steal (20:15)	8. Let him . . . no longer steal (4:28)
9. Do not bear false witness against your neighbor (20:16)	9. Put away falsehood (4:25)
10. Do not covet your neighbor's house, wife servants, animals, or anything else that is neighbor's (20:17)	10. Covetousness must not even be mentioned; no covetous person . . has any inheritance in the kingdom of God (5:3, 5)

Figure 7. Comparison Between Moses' and Paul's use of the Ten Words

Paul's usage of the fourth Word is perhaps the most obscure, with only brief encouragement to be thankful (5:4, 20) and guidelines for how to worship God (5:17-20). One reason for this might be that at least some of Paul's audience did not have a problem taking a day off. Perhaps that is why the seemingly unrelated admonishment to use time for God's kingdom was inserted. We cannot be certain. The *reason* for Paul's use of the fourth Word is more clearly stated. In Exodus, it is because God created us and all reality, and then rested; in Deuteronomy, it is because God rescued them from enforced seven-day-a-week slavery; now it is because Christ loved us and gave himself up for us (Eph 5:2), and rescued us from "24/7" enslavement to sin and other spiritual forces. Paul's usage of the rest of the Ten Words for the Ephesians is more explicit (see figure 7 above).

Whether or not Paul intended a one-to-one correlation, the Ten Words, as he explicates them, correspond to all the points in the Hellenistic worldview system (see figure 8 below). As such, they provide a more realistic framework for the Christian life than Hellenistic worldview systems, which are typically organized according to Greek categories.

What does this say about the worldview from which these new believers come? As the Hellenistic worldview was a human invention and convention, it was administered deterministically. Men were formed, made to be, to believe, to act in certain set ways.

All their lives they were taught the "party line": "think in terms of integration," "always try to accommodate theories and knowledge from different spheres with each other," "do not just accept things at face value, but look for deeper meanings that square with what you have been taught," "we need to keep striving for the transcendent ideal, the highest good," the transcendent (impersonal) cause or first principle which causes everything to exist. Increasingly, as the *Oikoumene* changed hands from Greek to Roman rule, and skepticism arose about the possibility of achieving the ultimate good, people began to believe instead that "happiness is a natural [achievable] end, not transcendent," and "man can make his way in the world despite the 'fates'."

EPHESIAN-HELLENISTIC WORLDVIEW	PAUL'S COVENANTAL INSTRUCTIONS
"God" is an abstract principle.	There is one body, one Spirit, one hope, one Lord one faith, one baptism, one God and Father of all, Who is over all, through all, and in all.
Behind everything is the Trancendent (impersonal) Cause/Principle which accommodates,integrates everything.	No longer live as Gentiles in futile thinking, blinded in understanding and separated from God's life because of ignorance in them due to hardened hearts.
Deterministic: men are formed, made to be/believe/act in certain ways.	Be thankful and sing to the Lord from heart. . . . Let no corrupting talk out of your mouth, only what is good for building up, fitting, giving grace to hearers.
'God' is immanent within reality; causes dualism.	Take care how you walk, not as unwise but as wise, making the most of the time for the days are evil.
Human invention/conventions rule, create reality.	Let all bitterness, wrath, anger,clamor, slander and malice be put away; obey/submit to one another in Christ.
Man can make his own way in the world despite fate.	Do not sin in your anger; do not let the sun go down on your anger.
Man can achieve Transcendent good and natural happiness.	Sexual immorality and all impurity must not even be spoken about among you; but live a life of love as Christ loved us and gave himself for us.
Man is the measure of the Cosmos.	Let the thief no longer steal; rather let him do honest work with his own hands so he may have something to share with those in need.
Broken/illogical metaphorical think-ing; allegorical reasoning is a hallmark.	Put away falsehood and let each one speak truth with his neighbor, for we reasoning are members of one another.
Need to keep striving for Transcendent Ideal, highest Good.	Covetousness is not to be spoken of; no covetous person has any inheritance in God's kingdom.

Figure 8 Comparison of Hellenistic and Covenantal Thinking

By contrast, the Ten Words were given by God in actual, historical encounters with the Jews, primarily, and were based on the way things actually are (i.e., God and Creation, man's nature and position, sin, and so on), contrary to the 'assumptions' behind their pagan worldviews (see figure 9). How do biblical givens, instructions, relate to the assumptions of those coming out of a Hellenistic worldview? Paul taught that man's errant thought processes amount to idolatry, the belief in false ways, if not gods (see Eph 4:17-19). The monistic mental habits of integration, accommodation, and allegorical reasoning are actually futile, the result of man's understanding being darkened by alienation from God due to the ignorance of his hardened heart.

GOD:
God is before and outside created reality. It can be said that he is greater than and "ontologically distinct" from creation, implying that there are different kinds of reality. (1)

CREATION:
God made man and everything; he made each according to its kind and set boundaries for the created order. It can be said that man and every thing are in (orderly) relation to God and to each other, not unrelated. (2)

GOD MADE MAN:
-of material elements and breathed into him the breath of life, and he became a living soul. It can be said that God values humans. (6)

-in his own image and likeness. It can be said that God desires relationship and that he relates to man in covenant. (5)

SIN:
God gave man a commission/stewardship over his creation, including people. Thus, it can be said that man is responsible/accountable to God. (4)

All of creation was under man's purview, except one tree bound up with the knowledge of good and evil. Man believed a lie (9) and disobeyed. All men sin/disobey/rebel; Augustine postulated that humans are unable not to sin. (10)

HISTORY/PROVIDENCE:
It can also be said that there is a beginning and an end of history, characterized by the actual consequences of sin, (8) and by God's actions to reveal himself, and to reconcile with man. (7) It can also be said that everything occurs according to God's wise and good/providential plan. (3)

Figure 9. Selected covenantal givens, with links to the Ten Words

Man has multiplied falsehoods:

1. Ideal-Material Dualism, that all reality--even "God"--is one, is a rejection of the first and second Words. Recent converts from Monism and Idealism needed to hear that there is "one God and Father of all, who is over all, through all and in all" (Eph 4:4). He is not an abstract principle, nor is he immanent within reality, but over it. God is over, through, and in all, instead of there being a dualism of transcendent ideal reality and an under-realm of matter that is merely an emanation of the real.

2. Allegorical Reasoning, using broken or illogical metaphors to reach moral conclusions, distorts the third and ninth Words. Hearers from a background of polyculturalism and the habit of confusing boundaries and fusing everything into one needed to be told that such reasoning is futile; they needed to hear that it is the result of having their understanding obscured by spiritual darkness and is due to their alienation from God (Eph 4:18-19).

3. The notion that man can achieve the transcendent good, or even natural happiness, to say nothing of perfection, that man can do anything he sets his mind to, and that man is the "measure of the cosmos" rejects the fifth and seventh Words. This natural human tendency, glorified by both Greece and Rome, is revealed to be man's declaration of autonomy from and rebellion against God. Paul reminded his hearers that they needed to put away falsehood and speak the truth to one another. He instructed the Ephesians to take steps to turn before it led them to the ultimate conclusion of taking another's life or killing them with words in order to maintain their autonomy (Eph 4:25-26).

4. Deterministic formation flies in the face of the third and fifth Words. When formation and the paideia system of education is deterministic to the point of doing violence to the conscience, it is thus a kind of murder. This type of conformism produces a suppressed anger that Jesus equated with murder as well (Eph 4:26, 31; Mt 5:21-22).

5.   Yearning for the ideal rejects Words seven, eight and ten. The universal push
     to achieve ultimate happiness, or the good, is an example of covetousness and
     sexual pleasure. It can attain such status as to seek the very place of God,
     and can also be seen as a form of theft. In fact, in a society built on
     achievement, stealing can exist in many forms: ideas, reputations, goodwill,
     to say nothing of one's neighbor's wife and goods (Eph 4:28; 5:3, 5).

Conclusions, Implications, and Recommendations

In conclusion, we are now reasonably certain that during the reign of Nero
the apostle Paul wrote a pastoral letter intended to encourage recently established
churches in the Roman province of Asia. The whole cultural scene of Paul's
written instructions to the new believers in Asia (Ephesians) focuses on God, the
One who rescued them and was now instructing them. Paul mentioned the
trinitarian God is mentioned more than any human person in the letter. Every
blessing they now had was set within his sovereign plan and purpose, conducted
through his gracious covenantal love and mighty power on their behalf. Paul's
paean of praise as prelude to his instructions served the same purpose for his
audience as the theophany did for the children of Israel in Exodus.

The context and worldview of these fledgling believers is hinted at in the
text and most certainly influenced Paul's instructions: life in a resource-rich area
with a temperate climate; urban dwellers in cities with an ancient polycultural
heritage; society based on slavery and driven by consumption and competition;
every activity tinged with family, state and personal religion; and all bound
together by neo-Stoic philosophy and the fates of astrology. Most spent their lives
in the vast economic enterprise feeding the Rome-centered demand for finished
goods, running the households or educating the sons of the privileged, or in the
government apparatus.

Paul, steeped in covenantal thinking, anchored by the Mosaic Ten Words,
encouraged those new believers to "put off" their old manner of life *in* their
context. The new covenant guidance that he offered paralleled Moses' Ten Words

point by point, and, at the same time, indirectly corresponded to the assumptions of their former worldviews, what the Gentiles around them still assumed: (1) "man can," stemming from the belief that man is both divine and beast--he can achieve whatever he sets his mind to and he can ruin himself and others in the process; (2) yearning, prompted by the ideal-material dualism, with their material reality a form of prison sentence compared to perfection; (3) allegorical and moralistic reasoning, a dualism that purported deeper reality lay behind the apparent; (4) inescapable and deterministic fate ruling everything; (5) all part of the one, all-encompassing reality of the monistic worldview.

Paul's insightful work cuts both ways. His epistle exposes the inadequate assumptions of the worldviews out of which the new believers came, and it demonstrates how a person steeped in covenantal thinking understands and engages those worldviews. This new thinking involves hearing the Word of the Lord, believing and repenting (confessing sin and getting rid of former practices, even if it hurts one's income). Paul battled the pervasive competition and consumerism with his own personal example of self-support and the revolutionary teaching that it was more blessed to give than to receive. These instructions are presented as a choice, not monistically. They are based on real, historical givens, not on assumptions or assertions.

Paul used much the same covenantal means used with the original giving of the Ten Words to instruct the Ephesians:

1. The power of God revealed the mystery of the gospel in Christ, Paul was bold in the face of an overwhelming and monolithic worldview, and extraordinary miracles accompanied his teaching and ministering.

2. The Holy Spirit called the Ephesians through Paul to covenant with God in faith in the Lord Jesus and in baptism.

3. All were seized with the "fear of the Lord" and held his name in high honor. Many believed, and openly confessed their evil deeds.

4. Throughout the New Testament period, long-term discipleship was conducted

by the apostolic band, including the pastoral oversight of Timothy, and later possibly John, Tychicus's visit, and Paul's visits and letters. Following the pattern of the Ten Words, his instructions were readily memorable.

Finally, Paul's Ten Words comprised covenantal instruction, an instrument of God's grace to these new believers. All heard, many believed, some experienced real change. As evidenced in the emotional elders' meeting at Miletus, strong, mutual love developed between Paul and those believers. At least a decade later, John commended their perseverance, while acknowledging the hold their worldview still had on them.

Paul's work proves a full-orbed stimulus to twenty-first-century Christians seeking to engage the culture. At the same time, this historic epistle encourages new believers to make the paradigm shift from old worldviews to a Hebrew-Christian, covenantal, way of life.

99

CHAPTER 6

CASE THREE: TWENTY-FIRST CENTURY
AMERICANS AND THE TEN WORDS

Introduction

This modern-day case study explores the worldview assumptions of two
loosely related cultural scenes in a major metropolitan area of the southeastern
United States. It also explores the role of the Ten Words (Commandments) to
help new believers learn the covenantal way of life, and it tests how the Ten
Words critique their former worldview assumptions.   The methodology of
questionnaire and analysis of responses is primarily employed. The questionnaire
is based on the critical analysis function of the Ten Words, using theory gleaned
from the two biblical case studies. By contrast, the biblical case studies in this
series utilize textual and historical analysis methodologies.

The research design, including case study methodology and research
protocol, follows this introduction of the third case study. Treatment of the data,
basically charts of Rasch-type conversion of textual responses to raw scores,
comes next. Findings follow, including a summary of the transcripts of responses,
simple statistical analysis, and a covenantal evaluation in light of the Ten Words.
Finally, conclusions, implications and recommendations are proffered.

Research Design

The methodology of this case study is based almost solely on responses to
a questionnaire designed to reveal the worldviews of these two related cultural
scenes. Its purpose is to strengthen and add to the theory that the Ten Words
prepare new believers to develop a covenantal way of life. To accomplish this the
protocol includes the following necessary elements: (1) define the research
question(s); (2) select the case and the population; (3) craft and test the protocols

and instrument; (4) conduct the study according to protocol; (5) protect the chain of evidence; (6) utilize both qualitative and quantitative methods; (7) conduct within-case and cross-case analyses; (8) triangulate by means of replication with other cases and by comparing with similar and conflicting precedent literature; (9) iterate continuously between collection, analysis, and theory; (10) reach closure.

Research question (RQ). By what means and to what extent have the Ten Words (Commandments) been used to disciple twenty-first-century Americans into the covenantal way of life, or to become functioning members of the covenant community? The second and third subsidiary questions are adapted as follows: What can be deduced from the transcript of responses to the worldview self-test about the worldview of the participants in the cultural scene? And why do they need instruction from the Ten Words? Subsidiary questions four and five are not addressed in this case.

Case. Two loosely related cultural scenes involving busy, professional twenty-first-century Americans.

Sources. Transcripts of responses to a blind, online worldview self-test from two groups, Group One (Unchurched), consisting of five respondents, and Group Two (Churched), consisting of eight respondents.

Craft instrument. First, exegesis uncovered key words, which were used in conducting two historical-textual case studies. From these, the subsidiary research questions were refined, and the issues which the Ten Words addressed were uncovered. These were then utilized in the construction of the protocol and testing instrument for this third case. Specific steps taken are described in appendix 2.

Summary of the Transcript

This study describes the worldview assumptions of two loosely related cultural scenes. One person, named Dave for the purposes of this report, straddles both scenes. In Group One, he is a fellow professional, specializing in computer management sales. This scene is populated with busy, traveling professionals across a variety of companies and research institutions in different cities. They intersect numerous times throughout the day by texting, Blackberry, and Linked In. Occasionally they have a get-together; otherwise their relationship is electronic for the most part. Group one respondents are his colleagues and unchurched friends. In group two, Dave and his family are active members of a medium-sized Presbyterian church. He and his wife also lead a weekly small group of six church couples, who, like themselves, are professionals serious about straddling their own professional and community scenes. They rotate homes to meet for fellowship and study. These church friends help each other out, watch each other's kids, and do things together as their busy lives allow. All of the respondents from group two are fellow church members with Dave.

What do the transcripts of actual responses of the two related groups tell about their worldviews? Group one consists of five unchurched respondents, and group two consists of eight churched respondents. The transcripts describe their expressed *values*, their views of the *nature of reality, power and influence, limits, trust and respect, life and death, loyalty or lust, the value of the person and work, integrity,* and *pleasure and appetite*. Together, their responses comprise, or at least indicate, their views of the world and reality.

We learn from group one that the pattern of their values is quite consistent and in line with what could be described as typical American values: God, family, friends, making a living, in that order of priority. Some add "contribute to society," "animals," "better myself." They ascribe allegiance to God, family, and country.

The transcript reveals one strong indicator of how group one regards the nature of reality: it is "*my* reality." Responses range from "[only] what I believe that I experience, perceive to exist," to a belief in God as ultimate reality. Two seem to believe both views simultaneously, and one thinks that "what is really real is the unseen, spiritual realm [and] that physical reality is like a dream."

Power and influence elicit unanimous "should" statements. Specifically, power or authority should "keep order," "provide guidelines," "serve as checks and balances . . . ensure no corruption."

Limits are, for some, based on the Ten Commandments and/or laws of the land. Others have a strong belief in "keeping things in proportion," "relative to the situation."

Trust and respect are almost unanimously viewed as "earned . . . through actions or alignment of beliefs." Some have clear priorities, distinguishing between family and friends, and everybody else and institutions. One asserts, "I can respect [those] who don't share my exact beliefs."

Almost all respondents in group one are adamant that life *is* a "huge value." While all opine "no has the right to take another life," some could allow for abortions, assisted suicides, and other "special situations." All but one believe in life after death.

The question of loyalty or lust is another with polarized responses. Most place a high value on marriage. Yet none can say that loyalty and lust are mutually exclusive. Most allow for lust, pornography, "window shopping" and "temporary indiscretions," as "not a reason to end marriages."

The value of the person and work elicit the most responses other than life and death. Responses include definite statements such as "I feel that my 'stuff' is the fruit of my good labor," and "I'm opposed to redistribution of wealth." At the same time, some made altruistic statements: "You work to make a positive impact and contribute above what's required," "We should help people that need help," "but I like it to be my choice." Several stated: "Theft, corruption, waste . . . drives me nuts," and "[I] hate these."

Integrity is very much defined by "self," according to this group. One remark, alluded to by others, is, "Because I define each of these categories [everything] either goes against my perceived values or support[sic] the values." For this category, they rate themselves "good" relative to others.

Pleasure and appetite are straight-forwardly identified *a la* "Maslow," while covetousness is denied. The rampant altruism ("serving others is my greatest pleasure," "I won't comprimise[sic] my morals," "I long for my kids to grow up to be responsible adults," "I don't think that I really covet anything that another has") may indicate a problem of face. Altogether, group one respondents are unsurprising in their worldview statements and exhibit a pattern that has become recognizable as typical of most twenty-first-century Americans.

In contrast, the eight respondents of group two describe themselves as believers and church members for at least ten years. Generally speaking, their responses approximate those of group one, although they are closer to, or to a greater degree attribute their learning from, the Bible. God is the highest value, followed by their spouse or family. God is also the main referent for life and death, loyalty or lust, and the value of the person and work.

The nature of reality elicited the most responses after the value of the person and work. Reality is "real and true," "actual," although they describe it variously. Some appear to express their beliefs somewhat dualistically: a "true original that this world was based on," an "ontic" and a phenomenal one. "Two forms of real reality . . . physical [and] spiritual" is somewhat closer to biblical.

The criteria for half of the responses for power and influence is God or the Bible. Half believe it "must be used for good end[s] through good means."

Limits are "important," "essential," "necessary," "a safeguard." For one respondent they are "the law."

This group's standard for trust and respect is the Bible. God has ordained it; "authority is granted by God." Less than half speak to trust or respect needing to be earned.

Life and death. As might be expected, God is the referent for most responses about life and death. This question also elicits the most "should" statements. Most believe in an afterlife, although they leave it unclarified; two explain it variously: "we persist," "the soul lives on."

As for loyalty or lust, marriage is highly valued and is based on the Bible. Loyalty and lust are mutually exclusive for at least half. "Lust is sin," to be "avoided" or "fenced."

The value of the person and work elicits the most responses. Again, God is the main referent for all but one. He "values each person;" he "ordains work;" value comes from him. Redistribution, at least by government, is "stealing" and "evil" and it "disheartens." Work is the means to owning property, and "one should work earnestly as for the Lord." "Theft, corruption, and waste" break the "commandment not to steal."

For the majority, integrity is something for which to strive. "There is a standard for justice, moral and ethical behavior." "I try to do what is right, kind, fair, honest and just." "I perceive lying, cheating, etc. to be sins," based on what the Bible says.

Pleasure and appetite are candidly admitted by most. One says covetousness is something to "battle," and that "these are all sins." One denies having any but spiritual desires. Covetousness is characterized materially by most ("comfort," "ease," and "wealth"), and spiritually by a few.

The overall pattern of group two definitely indicates an understanding of the world guided by Scripture. This is particularly obvious with regard to six categories: values, loyalty or lust, life and death, trust and respect, the value of the person and work, and power and influence. Admittedly, a few in this group reflect a mixture of biblical and other sources of learning as seen by their responses to limits, the nature of reality, integrity and coveting.

How is one to understand these patterns of responses? They may reflect the complexity and layers of what makes up the worldviews of contemporary Americans: how they were brought up, what they learned from the inculturation process of American popular culture and from the educational process, and what they have learned from the Bible or some other source(s) of choice. Some might assert that responses to such a questionnaire reflect how they are inherently. The responses also may be understood as a snapshot of one moment in the process of these peoples' lives. The responses may indicate that for some there is a trajectory away from God and learning Scripture, even though they may have had exposure to the Bible in their pasts. Other respondents appear to be in the process of exchanging or altering their native worldviews for biblical learning. At some point, these may have chosen to follow Christ and his teachings, including the Ten Words.

Treatment of Data

This study employs two generally accepted methods for establishing significance. The first is by far the more common. Significance is noted as the degree of deviation from the mean M of actual scores, and as such is an internal measure of comparison only--the degree to which the scores differ from each other. The other standard of significance usually noted is the degree of deviation from a fixed, external standard or criteria--a measure of anomaly, which is really a measure of theoretical deviation. In this study, that criteria is proximity either to Christian Scripture, in particular the Ten Words, or to other than biblical sources (see appendix 2). Both methods are employed in this study.

Simple Statistical Analysis

Rasch-type converted raw scores (tables 1, 3 and 4) are subjected to a simple statistical analysis, followed by within-case comparisons and then cross-case comparisons.

Within-group analysis. Thirteen respondents in groups one and two (table 1) provided 130 total responses. A response of 5, considered to be "alike," or the same as, the Ten Words or Scripture, is given the rank of 5 (table 2). 4 is proximate enough and given the rank of 4, and so on. The number of responses of group two have been adjusted to total 50 (column 4), the same as for group 1, for comparison sake. Total responses (column 6) reflect actual totals.

Table 1. Combined responses of groups one and two by group and respondent, and by question

Grp/ Resp.	Rank	Q1	Q2	Q3	Q4	Q5	Q6	Q7	Q8	Q9	Q10	Total	Aver.
							Questions						
2.6	1	5	5	5	4	4	4	5	5	4	5	46	4.6
2.7	2	5	4	4	4	5	5	5	4	4	4	44	4.4
2.1	3	5	4	4	4	5	4	5	5	4	4	44	4.4
2.5	4	4	4	4	3	4	5	5	5	4	4	42	4.2
2.8	5	5	4	3	3	3	4	5	4	4	4	39	3.9
2.2	6	4	4	5	3	4	4	4	2	2	3	35	3.5
1.1	7	4	2	3	4	4	4	5	4	2	4	35	3.5
2.4	8	3	2	3	3	4	4	4	3	3	4	33	3.3
2.3	9	4	1	3	3	4	4	3	4	4	1	31	3.1
1.4	10	4	1	3	2	3	4	3	3	2	4	29	2.9
1.5	11	4	1	3	4	2	1	2	4	3	4	28	2.8
1.3	12	3	2	3	3	3	1	1	3	3	2	24	2.4
1.2	13	3	2	3	2	4	1	3	2	1	2	23	2.3
Total		53	36	46	42	49	45	50	48	39	45	453	45.3
Average		5.3	3.6	4.6	4.2	4.9	4.5	5.0	4.8	3.9	4.5	4.5	4.5

Table 2. Summary of responses by proximity to biblical source

Proximi- ty rnk.	Group one		Group two		Totals	
	Responses	Percent	Responses	Percent	Responses	Percent
5	1	2	12	24	21	16
4	14	28	26	52	55	42
3	16	32	9	18	30	23
2	11	22	2	4	14	11
1	8	16	1	2	10	8
Totals	50	100	50	100	130	100

More than half of all responses (58%) are considered biblically derived, some directly from the Ten Words. Twenty-one (16%) are considered exactly biblical (alike), and 55 responses (42%) are sufficiently near to biblical to attribute influence. Ten responses (8%) are considered anthithetical to, or from sources completely other than, the Ten Words. Fourteen (11%) are considered sufficiently near to antithetical to attribute influence to learning opposed to biblical teaching, or from a distinctly different source. Together, 24 or almost twenty percent (18%) would be considered learning from some source other than the Bible. Thirty responses (23%) are sufficiently unclear or are a mixture such that it is not possible to determine how much influence was from biblical teaching or from other sources.

Table 3. Group one (unchurched) by question and respondent

	Respondents						
Question	1	2	3	4	5	Total	Average
Value (Q1)	4	3	3	4	4	18	3.6
Reality(Q2)	2	2	2	1	1	8	1.6
Power (Q3)	3	3	3	3	3	15	3.0
Limits (Q4)	4	2	3	2	4	15	3.0
Respect (Q5)	4	4	3	3	2	16	3.2
Death (Q6)	4	1	1	4	1	11	2.2
Lust (Q7)	5	3	1	3	2	14	2.8
Work (Q8)	4	2	3	3	4	16	3.2
Truth (Q9)	1	1	3	2	3	10	2.0
Covet (Q10)	4	3	3	4	4	16	3.2
Total	35	23	24	29	28	139	27.8
Average	3.5	2.3	2.4	2.9	2.8	13.9	2.8

In table 3, three of five respondents (numbers 2, 3 and 5) had two responses which could be considered learning from a completely other or anti-biblical source. One response from completely other sources was indicated by respondents 1 and 4. Additionally, all five respondents had other responses influenced by sources other than biblical. Altogether, 21 (42%) of the unchurched group responses are directly traceable to learning from non-biblical sources. Depending on one's background, this could be unexpected, given the heritage of American culture in "Christian" Europe,[43] or it could be expected, given the more

---

43 A major educational psychology text for undergraduates was typical just two generations ago in beginning its teaching with the Bible: Chpt. 2-Gn 22, Chpt. 3-The Ten

recent climate of diversity. On the other hand, only one respondent in this unchurched group had what could be considered an exactly biblical response (question #1, *loyalty or lust*). In addition, respondent 1 had four other responses that approximated a biblical response, and respondent 5 had four proximate responses. Altogether, 15 of the responses (30%) by unchurched respondents could be traceable to Christian learning.

Table 4. Group two (churched) by question and respondent

				Respondents						
Question	1	2	3	4	5	6	7	8	Total	Aver.
Value (Q1)	5	4	4	3	4	5	5	5	35	4.4
Reality (Q2)	4	4	1	2	4	5	4	4	28	3.5
Power (Q3)	4	5	3	3	4	5	4	3	31	3.9
Limits (Q4)	4	3	3	3	3	4	4	3	27	3.4
Respect (Q5)	5	4	4	4	4	4	5	3	33	3.3
Death (Q6)	4	4	4	4	5	4	5	4	34	3.4
Lust (Q7)	5	4	3	4	5	5	5	5	36	3.6
Work (Q8)	5	2	4	3	5	5	4	4	32	3.2
Truth (Q9)	4	2	4	3	4	4	4	4	29	2.9
Covet (Q10)	4	3	2	4	4	5	4	4	29	2.9
Total	44	35	31	33	42	46	44	39	314	39.0
Average	4.4	3.5	3.1	3.3	4.2	4.6	4.4	3.9	31.4	3.9

Group two (churched) (table 4). Of eighty responses for group two, 21 (16%) were fives, and 55 (42%) were fours, with more than half (58%) responding "biblically" (table 2). Conversely, the furthest respondent (3) from biblical learning in the churched group (table 4) also had two responses considered anti-biblical or deprived of biblical learning (*reality* and *coveting*). Respondent 2 had two fairly distant responses (*work* and *truth*) and 4 had one (*reality*). Altogether, 5 responses (6%) in the churched group had responses

---

Commandments and selected Proverbs, Chpt. 3-The Sermon on the Mount (Haimowitz and Haimowitz 1966).

distant from biblical truth, and together with 14 (18%) who were unclear as to their source, it signifies that almost one-quarter (24%) of the responses from the churched group are not clearly traceable to biblical learning (table 2). It is noteworthy that all of the unbiblical and 11/14 unclear responses (71%) come from just three of the eight respondents (38%).

Cross-group analysis (tables 1, 2 and 5). Group two respondents demonstrate more conviction and much less ambivalence than their group one counterparts. All but one alike to Scripture response (93%) was offered by group two. However, 64% of the ambivalent responses were from group one, reflecting the probability of a more mixed learning pattern. This can be seen by the familiar bell curve of responses from group one (table 2). Deviation from the actual mean *M* as a method can reflect inter-group comparisons (table 5).

Table 5. Deviations from actual mean (deviation 1) and theoretical mean (deviation 2).

Group	Respondent	Raw Score	Deviation 1	Deviation 2
2	6	4.6	+11	+16
2	7	4.4	+9	+14
2	1	4.4	+9	+14
2	5	4.2	+7	+12
2	8	3.9	+4	+9
2	2	3.5	0	+5
1	1	3.5	0	+5
2	2	3.3	-2	+3
2	3	3.1	-4	+1
1	4	2.9	-6	-1
1	5	2.8	-7	-2
1	3	2.4	-11	-6
1	2	2.3	-12	-7

The mean of actual responses (3.5) yields no further significant information than the simple ranking. Deviation from the theoretical mean of 3, however, yields the observation that all but two of group two (churched) fall above the mean, while all but one of group one (unchurched) fall below the mean. This underscores the observation that the ranges of responses for the two groups are clearly different, if not opposite. The fact that the range is almost evenly distributed around the actual mean, but skewed to proximity to biblical learning around the theoretical mean, may indicate the degree to which vestiges of biblical learning exist in the broader culture, or at least among the few unchurched with more scores above the mean.

Table 6. Derived total scores by rank

Respondent Assigned no.	Derived Scores	Percentage	Number of Respondents
2.6	920	90	1
2.7	880	80	3
2.1	880		
2.5	840		
2.8	780	70	3
2.2	700		
1.1	700		
2.4	660	60	2
2.3	620		
1.4	580	50	2
1.5	560		
1.3	480	40	2
1.2	460		

Derived scores obtained by assigning each response a numerical rank: 5=100, 4=80, 3=60, 4=40, 2=20; respondent numbers are the group number (1 and 2) plus respondent number.

To further clarify this difference, it can be seen on table 6 that six of eight (75%) respondents in group two (churched) have a derived score above 700. Both the scores and the percentage of the group with relatively high (proximate to biblical) scoring could be considered statistically significant. Respondent 6 scored 920/1000; respondents 7 and 1, 880, 5, 840, 8, 780, and 2, 750. Alternatively, all but one of group one (unchurched) had derived scores below 600: respondent 2, 460, 3, 480, 5, 560, and 4, 580.

Three values were identified as common to both groups (table 7). Concerning *values*, both groups had responses relatively proximate to biblical teaching. Similar scores in the unclear or mixed range regarding *power* in both groups indicate similar ambivalence about power and its use. Somewhat surprisingly, both groups scored similarly distant from biblical teaching on their understanding of the *nature of reality*, as well as of *honesty* and *truth*. More precisely, the churched group had two low scores in the same range as the unchurched group, lowering their total score.

Table 7 Key responses between the two groups

Proximity	Question
Proximate	Value
Medium	Power
Distant	Reality, Truth

Table 7 is based on raw scores in tables 3 and 4. First, the 10 questions (Q1-10) were ranked in three levels in relation to the Ten Words or biblical source: proximate to them, distant to them, or in a medium position between them. When the ranked questions from the two groups are placed parallel to one another, the common responses are noted in table 7.

Certain studies eliminate extreme high and low scores or cases of an extreme mode. However, it is this researcher's observation that the presence of one unchurched respondent indicating a relatively high degree of scriptural influence, and of two churched respondents indicating resistant beliefs to Scripture, or divergence from it, underscore the actual diversity, at least in this contemporary American population. Therefore, these extreme scores should not be treated specially (eliminated) for purposes of observation, which is the principal function of simple statistics.

Interestingly, the respondent most proximate to biblical truth in the unchurched group ranked closer than tow in the churched group. Furthermore, the lowest three in the churched group have almost identical scores as the the tope three in the unchurched group. On the surface these three churched respondents seem to be normal believers. However, their responses belie a worldview that is a mixture of fundamentally different approaches to life.

Covenantal Analysis

Three of five from group one (unchurched) claim to derive some guidance from God, the Bible, or even the Ten Commandments (figure ten below). However, the extensive use of the first person singular, together with words such as "perceive," "define," "believe," "live," "acquire," indicate that these respondents actually view the self as the one who decides what to believe, how to live life, what is of value, and so on.[44] The individual, this world, society, and one's family, friends and job dominate the scene, certainly not God. In other words, it appears that this scene is really all there is for them, at least the only thing of which they can be certain. From their perspective, if such a god can exist, it does not appear ontologically distinct, nor prior to, or over, created reality; rather, it appears to be immanent within, or a transcendent abstraction.

On the other hand, for group two (churched), it can be said from the transcript that God holds *a*, possibly *the*, central place in their responses. Altogether, there were seventy-eight mentions of deity or Scripture in eighty responses. God is mentioned multiple times in response to all ten questions, principally on the question of *life and death*, and also concerning *man and his work*. God was mentioned by almost 90% of the respondents from group two for three questions: *values, man and his work,* and *life and death*. God was this

---

44 Van Til observes: "The finite mind cannot thus, if we are to reason theistically, be made the standard of what is possible and what is impossible" (1955, 39).

GROUP ONE (UNCHURCHED) WORLDVIEW	GROUP TWO (CHURCHED) WORLDVIEW
1. Values family (4/5) friends (3/5) God (3/5) work (3/5)	God (7/8) family (6/8) values (3/8)
2. Reality natural/scientific, what I perceive (3/5) dualistic/pantheistic (3/5) agnostic re: Ultimate Reality (2/5)	real, true, actual (3/8) dualistic(?): true original & this (1,3); ontic & phenomenal (7); physical & spiritual (8)
3. Power should be/oughtness (4/5) use for good (4/5)	criteria: God/Bible (4/8) purpose (4/8); good means & end (4/8)
4. Limits necessary/good for order/protect (4/5) but flexible/proportionate use (4/5) market driven (1/5); 10 Commandments (1/5)	important,essential, necessary(5/8) + law (1/8) + safeguard (1/8)=(7/8)
5. Respect earned (5/5) basis: God/Bible (2/5); other (1/5)	standard: Bible (5/8) God ordained, gives authority(3/8) earned (3/8)
6. Life based on belief, should believe (4/5) life = value (4/5) OK: abortion (2/5), assisted suicide (1/5) afterlife (2/5); maybe/agnostic (3/5); nothing (0/5)	based on God (7/8) afterlife (5/8): we persist, soul lives on (2/8); life & death un-clarified (6/8)
7. Loyalty or Lust ≠ mutually exclusive (4/5) OK/understandable: lust, porno, adultery (4/5)	marriage (7/8); God revealed (4/8) mutually exclusive (4/8); ≠ (1/8) lust = sin (3/8); avoid/fence (3/8)
8. Work redistribution: NO (4/5) should contribute to society (4/5) work -> property (4/5)	God(7/8): values each (5/8); ordains work (4/8); theft, etc. = sin (3/8) work -> property (3/8) redistribution: evil(3/8); sin(1/8) disheartens (1/8)
9. Integrity what I define/believe (3/5) fixed (3/5); shades (2/5)	strive for (5/8) based in God/Bible (3/8) deceit = sin (3/8)
10.Covet desire: acquire by work (4/5) things (3/5); marriage, kids, peace, happiness (2/5)	comfort, ease, wealth (3/8) admit covet. (6/8); battle (1/8); no desire (1/8) materialize (5/8); spiritualize (2/8)

Figure 10. Contemporary American worldviews compared

group's highest value on question one. Furthermore, God and the Bible were mentioned as key for *power and influence*, question three, and God ordained m*arriage*, question seven. However, attribution to God or the Bible for questions on *integrity*, *authority*, *respect*, and *reality* seriously tapered off. Once again, the ambivalent responses were due mostly to three relatively distant from biblical learning.

The disparate worldview responses of both groups reflect ways of life superficially similar, but fundamentally quite different. Group one's responses reflect a mixture between two fundamentally different ways of life. On the surface, these people are honest, hardworking, moral people with a strong view of marriage, family, belief in the necessity and good of limits, the value of life and the belief (without having proof or needing it, so it would seem) that this life is not all there is. Most appear to be acquainted with the Bible and a few probably attend church occasionally. Most claim to believe in, or try to believe in, God (5/5: believe or try to believe in *life after death*, question 6; 3/5: God is the highest *value*, 1; 2/5: God sets *limits*, 4; 2/5 God, or the Bible, is the basis for *respecting authority*, 5).

In other words, group one respondents have a christianist basis for their lives, a mixture, or synthesis, of biblical givens and other worldview assumptions. They hold to naturalistic opinions; two or three are expressly dualistic in that they hold to a naturalistic view of this life. Simultaneously, these same respondents hold to a belief in God and an afterlife. One response is an outright Eastern mystical belief, expressing a certainty of the unseen world with the claim that the material world is like a dream. This group holds to standards, to bases, other than scriptural, for what they perceive as two distinct realms of reality.

The concept of God, specifically, for almost all of group one, appears to be abstract. He is viewed as a transcendent principle or cause, and/or immanent within reality, or reality is perceived as immanent within God. This perspective results in or, at minimum allows, a kind of dualism in which there exist two realities side by side, or one reality with two sides. The physical side of reality is viewed scientifically and separate from, and without affecting, a spiritual understanding of an unseen side to reality, and/or vice versa. This is characteristic of what is referred to as postmodernism, in which boundaries between ideas, facts and realities are porous, and other interpretations, or even realities, are implied. This is in opposition to the more rigid definitions, boundaries, and either/or thinking that has characterized modernism.

Group one's "should" statements seem to suggest the "oughtness" of determinism more than the historical reality of biblical givens (e.g., "I should not compromise," "should strive to respect those who want and try," "power and authority should be used as guidelines . . . . . benevolently . . . . to help . . . . to do the wise thing," "should help others," "should punish wrong-doers," "there should be balance"). Their strong statements of belief, definitions, and so on appear to indicate that they themselves, or human invention and convention, determine reality, or at least the understanding or meaning of it (e.g., "only what I believe," "I define what reality is," "who I want to be," "I don't like those who don't follow mine," "I believe that," in addition to the "what should be" statements above). Man, in this worldview, is the measure of reality.

However, their belief in both determinism and human invention or convention appears to be contradictory. On the one hand, they appear to believe that *in the nature of things* everything should be for the good (already), and everyone should work for the good of all, while at the same time, they believe that one should keep trying, keep striving to achieve these ideals. It seems that these unchurched respondents believe in some kind of cosmic balance scales (Bavinck 1981, 45, 131), that there is an equilibrium to be maintained, or that factual reality is affectable by human intentions or actions ("reality is what I believe exists," "I don't believe in hard rules," "I believe in the law of equilibrium . . . all aspects of life go up and down around each person's equilibrium chart," "I believe in the invisible hand of the market," and so on).

The researcher must be careful not to apply a stricter standard to churched believers as if they should "know better." The Ten Words critique everyone, churched and unchurched alike, whatever our worldviews actually are, not what might be wished. When one compares the responses of group two (churched) to specific teaching of the Ten Words or other similar Scripture texts, more than half responded in ways that can be attributed directly to scriptural learning , including some that specifically refer to the Ten Words. Over 75% of the scriptural responses were from this group. Group two had a higher degree of conviction and much less ambivalence than group one. Almost all responses to f our questions clearly demonstrated biblical learning: predominately regarding *loyalty or lust*, then, *values*, then attitudes towards *life and death*, and the fourth, r*espect*.

Aside from these four questions, the other six questions show wider divergence. The pattern of assumptions was similar for both groups for *power, respect, the value of the person and work,* and *coveting.* Yet, group two consistently attributed their beliefs to God or Scripture compared to group one's attribution to 'other' or indeterminate sources: *power* is for good. Group one's source is indeterminate or oughtness (80%); group two's is the Bible (50%). *Respect* is to be earned, based on the Bible, for 40% of group one, and for 63% of group two. *Work* is good, for group one due to personal opinion (100%), and for group two, because God ordained it (88%). *Coveting* is implicitly admitted by group one, to be acquired by work (80%), while group two admitted to committing, equating it with sin (75%).

However, clear indications emerge that three from this group, although describing themselves as believers and church members for at least ten years, indicate by their responses that they have not learned, or have disregarded or not believed, biblical teaching. Interestingly, the respondent most proximate to biblical truth in the unchurched group ranked closer than two in the churched group. Furthermore, the lowest three in the churched group have almost identical scores as the top three in the unchurched group.

On the surface these three churched respondents seem to be normal believers. However, their responses belie a worldview that is a mixture of fundamentally different ways of life. This is most apparent with regard to questions of *truth*, *coveting*, *reality*, *limits*, and *person and work*. On the surface these three seem to be normal believers. Some of their responses were biblical. At the same time, all three had responses to these questions that approximate those of the unchurched respondents. In summary, it appears that two-thirds of group two respondents have learned their worldview from Scripture, yet one-third have constructed their worldview by fusing biblical with non-biblical sources. Distinctly non-biblical responses occur in response to questions about *reality*, 2, *truth*, 1, *person and work*, 1, and *coveting*, 1. It is unverifiable whether these are fixed views or in process of maturation.

One disturbing variable is that although clearly less ambivalent than group one, nevertheless, more than one-third of the responses from group two are unclear as to the source of their learning. This could be attributable either to poor biblical learning or to preferences for other sources of learning. Alternatively, this could be attributed to some ambivalence felt when faced with these questions, or to wording of the questions that may appear vague or confusing.

The churched group's responses also reflect a fair amount of moralism. This is particularly evident in the question regarding *integrity*. Responses include "attempt," "try and expect," "strive," "aspire and desire," "keep by willpower," "falling short," "sinning." Altogether one-fourth of the group two responses could be considered moralistic, relatively speaking. From group two, *life and death* also elicits two moralistic responses, *integrity*, 2, and *work*, 1.

On the issue of moralism, almost the same percentage of moralistic responses as among the churched group also exists among the five unchurched group respondents. However, the unchurched group's moralism, by contrast to the churched group, is directed more towards others in power, than to self.

Throughout this covenantal evaluation, the churched group responses appear consistently more proximate to biblical learning than to other sources or ambivalence. The range of their scores may reflect the struggle to keep their covenantal commitment in the face of a broader cultural worldview approximating the unchurched responses.

Conclusions and Recommendations

Case Study Three is a qualitative study of contemporary Americans. A blind, online "Worldview Self-test" questionnaire was administered to gain responses for ten worldview categories. Though not explicitly the Ten Words (Commandments), the "Worldview Self-test" is, nonetheless, based on them. As such, the ten questions identify key assumptions and beliefs, including real-life attitudes and behaviors. Furthermore, the questions differentiate between biblical and other sources of learning, and indicate certain tendencies. Conclusions are based on the responses of thirteen participants.

The cultural scene studied consists of two loosely related sets of professional people in a Southeastern metropolitan area of the United States. Groups one and two are loosely related in terms of where they live and work, overlapped by a common participant. The respondents in both sets superficially share similar American values: God, family, honesty, hard work, basic morality, a high view of marriage and family, the value of life, and belief in an afterlife. However, this brief study reflects two fundamentally different, though sometimes overlapping, sets of assumptions for their sometimes similar opinions and beliefs.

Clearly, biblical learning influences the bulk of their responses. Unidentified other sources provide a strong alternative, especially for the unchurched group and a few members of the churched group. Nevertheless, the responses indicate vestiges of biblical learning remaining in the broader culture (see Schaeffer 1985, 131-2) for at least a few unchurched respondents. Additionally, ambivalence shown by the nearly one third unclear or mixed responses probably indicates a mixture of sources for learning, primarily among the unchurched group. Just as clearly, God is the key referent for the churched group, while the self, and possibly conventional wisdom, is the key referent for the unchurched group.

Analysis of the responses from the questionnaire is unable to answer the subsidiary questions: (SQ4) By what means can the Ten Words be used to instruct the respondents? (SQ5) To what extent can covenant or the Ten Words be used to instruct the respondents: in what ways are they instruments of grace, and what is their function in this instruction? Neither can the analysis fully describe details of the cultural scenes in terms of lifestyle and behaviors such as the other two case studies in this series were able to provide based on the available transcripts and other etic observations. Nevertheless, worldview theorists (Kearney, Hiebert) argue that worldview should be able to predict behaviors.

Further studies of this type to attempt to replicate these kinds of findings are encouraged. Additionally, further qualitative and quantitative studies of these two cultural scenes is encouraged to validate or refute these preliminary findings. Questions that might be addressed include (1) Should the variety of worldview differences in the population in general be expected to be similar within the American church? (2) How do different factors such as generation, background before becoming a member, etc. affect responses? and (3) What in societal worldview or area of life affects difficulty in believing biblical teaching?

CHAPTER 7

TREATMENT OF DATA AND FINDINGS

Data are treated according to accepted theory in the following pertinent fields: biblical ontology, worldview theory, and integrative/qualitative research methodology theory. Two areas of theory emerged, or are seen to be complementary with precedent theory: (1) a comprehensive covenantal theory, and (2) mutually complementary covenantal ethnohermeneutic and integrative/ qualitative research methodology theories. Utilizing these theories, three cases/cultural scenes are studied. Findings from a comparison of text transcripts between two uses of the Ten Words with two biblical populations, and findings from a hands on contemporary use of a Ten Words-based questionnaire with a contemporary population of two related scenes, are presented in tables and other graphical media accompanied by textual explanation. Alternative interpretations of meaning are included as well. Findings are generalizable to broader theory and not to other populations.

Research outcomes are dependent on real data, and they are dependent, as well, on human understanding of the data. The researcher allows the transcripts to speak for themselves and respondents to control what is known about them, reflecting their dignity as created subjects. Since peoples' responses to surveys and other response tools is expected to reflect their actual intent to communicate, their answers and comments may even include face posturing and even prevarication.

In the field of biblical ontology, covenant theory, in particular, is studied and applied to other areas of theory and to the case studies. Covenantal ethnohermeneutics, an emerging field of study, is derived partially from this study. Covenantal theory combines Jewish ontic hermeneutics and Reformed Protestant theory to yield four main points of theory. First, *God creates Creation*.

This is the basis for everything, explains reality, provides for all knowledge, just as Averbeck notes that *covenant* was pervasive on several levels in the Ancient Middle East. Also, God *creating* implies an ontological gap, yielding the ultimate human crisis of separation from God, and implies that God comes to us, that we cannot reach him. Second, *Mediator and renewal* is necessary and singular, accomplished by Jesus Christ's real life, death and resurrection, thereby fulfilling God's promise, extending grace, and "calling" humans to a covenant relationship. Third, *covenant relationship* requires prior willingness to hear and cooperate, is only possible by God's grace and repentance, consists of a mutual bond, a commitment of love and loyalty, and includes ultimate allegiance to God. Fourth, the *covenantal way of life* ensues from the Covenant, and is a framework of purpose and righteousness for every area of life. It involves fulfillment, that is, recognition of the authority of the text (Scripture) and working to be part of its fulfillment. This full-orbed theory thus is related to and critiques every other theory.

In the field of worldview theory, worldview analysis is studied and critiqued by covenantal theory. Highlighting five areas of need for further research, this critiqued version of worldview analysis provides the second portion of theory for covenantal theism, or ethnohermeneutics. The five areas to further research the validity of worldview theory are (1) the possibility of a universal meta theory of human perception and categorization of phenomena; (2) visualization radically objectifies reality; (3) mental conceptualizations determine or outrank reality; (4) worldview assumptions are tacit and therefore neutral; and (5) worldview is predictive of human behavior and vice versa.

In the field of research methodology theory, integrative and qualitative research methodology theory is studied, particularly these aspects: overall design, replication, triangulation and case study, including qualitative interviewing. This body of theory is compared favorably with the emerging covenantal ethnohermeneutic theory, deriving seven mutually complementary theories/

methods: (1) tacking & iteration in conduct of research (Maxwell) parallels creational relationality and can be likened to the approach of Hebrew-biblical; (2) documented warrant (Creswell) takes reality seriously, as does Scripture; (3) real-life bases for case study (Yin) parallels biblical concreteness; (4) doing biblical case study (Gangel) lets texts speak for themselves; (5) qualitative interview approach gives public voice to respondents (Bellah), and thus parallels the biblical "warts and all" approach; (6) the practice of triangulation (Larsen) parallels the biblical wisdom approach, and the principle of two or three witnesses (Dt 17; Mt 18; 2 Cor 13); and (7) actual case basis plus replication strengthens theory (Creswell), which can be an application of the universality of biblical concrete case approach. In addition, Reid's assertion that covenant can critique culture provides a warrant in the literature for asking the research question and conducting this study.

Next, theory, particularly methodological, is utilized to examine the actual data in the cases, yielding rich findings, some corroborative of the theory. First, the Old Testament case study of the liberation of Israel as a nation and the renewal of the Covenant under Moses yields at least six findings:

1. God was the focus of the entire episode. Every part of the setting and everything that occurred was set within God's sovereign plan and purpose. What occurred on Mt. Sinai was a fulfillment of God's promise and was to Israel's benefit.

2. Moses' transcript describes how the Israelites were in extreme distress and could not save themselves. God's people had to be liberated first, followed by renewing the Covenant.

3. Close examination of the stipulations and case laws uncovers evidence that, most likely, their behavior was far different than that of the God with whom they were in covenant. Normal humans, the Israelites faced every deprivation and new experience with fear and unbelief, which, in fact, prevented the generation liberated from slavery from entering the Promised Land.

4. The centerpiece of the entire biblical scene was the Ten Words of God—the creative core of a covenantal way of life. In fact, the Ten Words themselves are the chief theory and findings of this case study: (1) God is the One, Unique, who rescues you from what you yourself cannot escape; render to him alone exclusive loyalty; (2) give God glory in everything; craft no icons or idols; (3) trust all your ways with all your heart to God; (4) set aside every seventh day for God, to rest in his grace; (5) honor and respect parents and all authority; (6) no murder; treat others as you want to be treated; (7) no adultery; keep loving only your first love (wife); (8) no taking what is not yours; do not defraud others; (9) no lying or favoritism; and (10) no coveting; be content with what God provides.

5. These Ten Words were accompanied by wondrous and unmistakable signs of deity--clear indications that God was dealing directly with his people. The Ten Words revealed what God was like, and not like. They tested the people to see if they would obey--a sign of faith (they failed). The Ten Words created hope of a new humanity. They set boundaries around what a covenant people were to be like. They explained love in action. Finally, the Ten Words were to be learned in order to teach others: their children and outsiders.

6. The Ten Words and succeeding 613 case laws were a body of authoritative givens, the instructional stipulations of the Mosaic Covenant. These words carved in stone appear to be intended to parallel the character of God himself. As a people, the children of Israel were called (*Sh'ma*, Dt 6) to love the Lord with all their being, to love one another, and to pass on their covenantal way of life to others.

Second, the Ten Words are found to be in full use after the pivotal inauguration of the New Covenant. The case study of Paul to the Ephesians adapted the Ten Words to a new set of believers and members of the covenant Community--the Gentiles. Paul's communication to them follows the same covenantal structure of the renewal of the Covenant through Moses. Note four parallels: (1) a paean of praise to God and every blessing for the Ephesians was part of his covenantal plan "before the Creation," paralleling God's theophany and covenantal plan for Israel; (2) the Ephesians (Gentiles) were without God and excluded from the covenants of promise and citizenship, just as the Israelites were enslaved in Egypt: both were without hope; (3) the Ephesians were called, saved, made alive "in Christ," to put off the old and put on the new, just as the Israelites were renewed in the Covenant centuries prior; and (4) having been rescued, the new Gentile believers were given the same instructional stipulations, even though communicated in different order and wording, as the Ten Words had been given to Israel.

In addition, the Covenant, anchored by the Ten Words, critiqued the Gentiles' old worldview assumptions in radical fashion, yielding five findings: (1) their monistic mental habits of integration, accommodation, and allegorical reasoning were futile; (2) the dualistic notion that a deeper reality lay behind the apparent was not telling the truth; (3) the attitude of "man can"--that he can achieve whatever he sets his mind to--stems from the belief that man is both divine and beast, and can ruin himself and others in the process, resulting in murderous thoughts if not the deed; (4) yearning, actually covetousness, is prompted by ideal-material dualism, whereby our material reality is a form of prison sentence in comparison to the perfect ideal; (5) inescapable and deterministic fate ruling everything can lead to rebellion and bitterness; and finally, (6) these are all part of the one, all encompassing reality of the monistic worldview, denying the God who is unique, and over, in and through all created reality.

Case study three is possible only because of the findings from the two biblical cases, principally: (1) the Ten Words were given by God with specific didactic roles; (2) their role in covenantal thinking and principles could be adopted by Paul for a different audience and still perform the same function as the original Ten; (3) they cut both ways—they were instructional stipulations of what God is like and what his being in the midst of his people entailed, and also served as indicators of why the old worldview assumptions are *not* like God, nor acceptable for fellowshipping with him.   Therefore, the inherent power and authority of the Ten Words to critique culture is the assumption for the Worldview Self-test administered to thirteen volunteer respondents in a metropolitan area in twenty-first century America.

Volunteered responses yield findings similar to findings in the two biblical case studies. These are demarcated by the churched, who evidence at least some instruction from God's stipulations, and the unchurched, who express evidence of some other sources of worldview mixed with vestiges of the Ten Words. One, God and the Bible are mentioned in almost all responses of the churched group, while the self and conventional wisdom are the referents of choice for the unchurched group. Two, all the responses of the churched group are above the fixed mean (mid-point between Scripture and some unidentified alternative source of worldview conviction), while all but one of the unchurched group fall below the mean. Three, all of the unchurched respondents exhibit a mixture of sources, whereas only the most distant two or three of the churched group exhibit another source from biblical. Four, some responses from the unchurched parallel the following worldview assumptions Paul critiqued in his letter to the Ephesians: (a) synthetic-integration mindset; (b) moralism as an end-product of allegorical reasoning; (c) "man can" thinking with the self as reference point; (d) yearning for the ideal or perfect; (e) naturalism (monism), with God either being denied or seen as a pantheistic ally immanent within reality.

Two further steps, suggested by the research methodology theory, are required to complete an analysis of the findings: replication and triangulation. Yin's emphasis on replication is underscored by Eisenhardt 1989. The theory is that either actual replication (e.g., three of three cases) or theoretical replication (at least one contrary reading out of three, deemed replication for theoretical reasons) serves to strengthen the reliability of theory. Replication is more internal corroboration, whereas triangulation is more external, gaining corroboration in this case among parallels found in three different bodies of precedent literature, and between literature theory and the findings from the case studies, two of which are historical and literary, and one that is contemporary and interview driven.

The three cases differ, yet have similarities. The Old Testament case concerns the re-constitution of an ancient Semitic people as a nation. The New Testament case is the inclusion of Gentiles for the first time. They were Greco-Roman, polycultural urbanites on the scene a millennium and a half after Mt. Sinai. Yet, these two cases exhibit the similar challenge of limited access: only transcripts of the actual events exist, and they are in languages and cultures other than the researcher's. By contrast, the third case study is contemporary, the transcript the result of volunteer responses to a blind on-line questionnaire crafted and administered by the researcher himself. In the latter instance, some of the researcher's worldview assumptions influence the instrument and process.

Actual replication consists in both the similar structure of each case, as well as in the findings. The structure is replicated in all three cases: (1) the same research question(s); (2) the use of the Ten Words in all three; (3) a similar protocol used for all three; (4) a similar organizational structure for the written report.

Replications also occur in the findings. One, God is the focus of all three cases, and his covenantal structure is evident in the theory, for example by plan, promises and fulfillment, and so on. Two, all three cases have populations that have very different characteristics than God, and are without hope of rescue from their sinful conditions. Some are now new believers and in need of instruction regarding how to be in covenant with God and with each other. Three, in each case the descriptor "mixture" is mentioned: the Israelites were a mixed company of some who were faithful and some who were unfaithful, during and after the Mt. Sinai episode; Paul warned the Ephesians to avoid mixing with their former way of life; and the contemporary churched group shows signs of mixing biblical learning with other worldviews.

Four, the Ten Words are the core for biblical learning in each case. Note also, rather than being used literally, their wording, order and, to some degree, worldview influence/issue they address has been adapted. Fifth, the Ten Words not only give parameters in each case for what God is like, but, in describing what he is not like, they critique the worldviews from which each population comes. Sixth, many of these worldview assumptions are similar: unbelief/lack of trust in God, what they valued and gave allegiance to, the use of power to overcome life's challenges, their views of the nature of reality and truth, actual behavioral consequences, for example, in terms of not treating others fairly, lack of respect, rebellion and bitterness, falsehood in their most intimate loyalties, and so on. For these reasons, substantial actual replication among all three cases can be demonstrated, despite the superficial *dissimilarities* of textual distance for the biblical cases and hands on actuality for the contemporary case, and despite dissimilarities of methodology.

Triangulation among the three bodies of literature and the findings demonstrates further parallels. One, covenantal literature found God, the Creator, to be the basis for everything and all knowing, just as God was revealed to be the focus of both biblical scenes as well as that of the contemporary churched scene. Two, descriptors of the Covenant found in the literature are also found in the three cases: keeping promise, mediation by God to change their situations, grace, comprising all of life, bond of loyalty and love, and so on. Three, the real-life bases for case study, letting texts speak for themselves, and letting respondents have their own voice, are reflected in the "warts and all" reporting of the biblical transcripts, and encouraged by the blind and voluntary nature of the contemporary respondents. These factors reflect a high correspondence with the truth, with the way things actually are, another characteristic of comprehensive covenantal theory.

Four, Reid's assertion that covenant can critique culture was demonstrated by covenantal critique of surrounding worldviews in the Old Testament case, particularly by extrapolating from case laws attitudes and behaviors the Israelites must have had, by Paul's covenantal critique of Greco-Roman worldview assumptions, and by the clear differentiation evinced by the Worldview Self-test between responses by the churched and unchurched groups also demonstrate the critical power of the Ten Words.

Five, the triangulation of Larsen approximating the perspectivism of biblical wisdom is demonstrated by the similarities of issues and worldview assumptions that emerge in different expressions and perspectives from the three extremely diverse cultural scenes: Israelite, Greco-Roman and American. For example, all were without God and without hope of release from three very different situations: Israelites enslaved to Egyptians and sin, Ephesians caught in the Roman imperial commercial "combine" and sin, and American unchurched trapped in unbiblical, and therefore, incoherent worldview assumptions and practices such as pornography, sexual dalliances, and abortions. All thought they could practice a kind of "designer religion," dabbling in various practices and assumptions from worldviews around them while claiming to be loyal to God alone. The Israelites crafted "golden calves" and cavorted with religious prostitutes. The Ephesians reasoned allegorically to moralize ascetic practices in order to be perfected. And Americans believe that if they are altruistic they will gain merit.

Split-level living is exhibited in the following examples between what each claimed to believe and their actual behavior. The Israelites yearned for the "cucumbers and leeks" of Egypt when faced with deprivation and were fearful when faced with unknowns, immediately after being rescued through the Red Sea. The Ephesians clamored, slandered, were unforgiving, and exhibited other malicious evidences of rebellion against the monistic system, not long after "fearing and honoring God." And, Americans jealously guard what they work hard for (unchurched), and lust after "pretty things" and manipulate people and situations to achieve them (churched). These behaviors uncover the ultimate human crisis caused by the ontological gap between Creator God and created humans and demonstrate the necessity of Christ's "It is finished" on the Cross and the need of repentance on our part.

These examples come to awareness principally because of the Scripture's insistence on "warts and all" reporting. This is reflected in textual case studies that allow the texts to speak for themselves and by the qualitative interviewing of the blind questionnaire that encourages voluntarism and transparency of response.

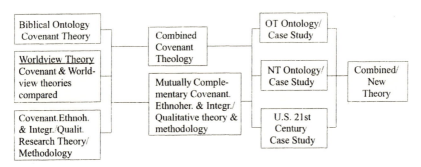

Precedent theory->Derived/combined theory+Case Study theory=Theory closure

Figure 11 Theory development

Theory from the three theory areas and data from the three cases have been examined and compared. Substantial replication and triangulation has been found and specific examples noted. A tentatively new three-part theory is noted as cohering throughout.

One, covenant pervades all of life: a full-orbed theory was developed from Jewish ontic hermeneutics and Reformed Protestant covenant theory. It was noted as the operational key to all three cases: the covenant renewal through Moses, the covenantal approach of Paul and covenant renewal with the Ephesians, and the covenantal approach of this researcher to the contemporary case.

Two, because it pervades on several levels, if less apparently today than in the Ancient Middle East, covenant also critiques other worldviews. The researcher used covenant theory to critique both worldview theory and integrative/ qualitative research methodology theory, resulting in a covenant theory and covenantal ethnohermeneutic theory which includes an area of complementarity with the research methodology.

Three, the Ten Words are the creative core of covenant as a means to induct new members and critique their old worldviews. The transcripts of the Old and New Testament cases reveal this functional role occurring in all three cases: in the authoritative giving of the Ten Words by God himself from Mt. Sinai as covenant authoritative stipulations, by Paul's use of the Ten Words to include the Ephesians in the covenant community, and by references to the Ten Words in the responses of the contemporary churched group. A vestige could be identified in one unchurched response, identifying the Ten Commandments specifically as the basis for boundaries. Finally, the use of the Worldview Self-test, based on the Ten Words, demonstrated their ability to critique worldview, or at least to demarcate what was biblical learning and what was learning from other sources.

CHAPTER 8

CONCLUSIONS AND RECOMMENDATIONS

This research has been concerned with challenges faced by the Church, particularly in the West, to provide a "reason for its hope." The Ten Words (Commandments) were examined for their role in inducting and instructing new members in faith and covenantal living. Five questions were asked of three case studies: ((1) What or who is the focus of the case study? (2) What does the transcript itself report of the participants' former way of life (worldview), and what covenantal instruction from the Ten Words is needed? (3) What does the Covenant entail, of what does the covenantal way of life consist, and how is this new way different from their old way of life? (4) By what means are the Ten Words used to instruct the participants? (5) To what extent are the Covenant or the Ten Words used to instruct the participants and in what ways are they instruments of grace?

Regarding the focus of the case studies, God and the accompanying blessing of his covenant were seen to be the focus of both biblical case studies and of the contemporary churched group. Question two seeks to discover the former way of life and need of the participants. Similar parallels are found to exist in the two ancient transcripts (biblical text) and in the transcript of responses from the contemporary case. In all three cases the participants were experiencing some kind of real enslavement from which they could not extricate themselves. Worse, they were distant, if not apart, from God. From the descriptors, all bore little resemblance in values, character, and behavior to God, and all were in need of learning a new way of life.

The third question asks the differences between the old and new ways of life. Responses indicate a sharp demarcation in all three instances between the

Covenant and covenantal way of life, and lives based on other worldviews. Third-person descriptions by covenant members of life based on other worldviews in the biblical cases, emerges from actual self descriptions of the contemporary unchurched group.

The fourth question concerns the role of the Ten Words in covenantal instruction. The Ten Words are the centerpiece and core in all three cases. In the Old Testament case they are the authoritative instructions for being in covenant with God given directly by God himself. Paul adapts the full Ten Words for the Gentiles of the first century A.D., although in other words. And, the researcher bases a worldview questionnaire on the Ten Words for the contemporary case.

The fifth question concerning the use and nature of the Ten Words instruction could not be applied to the contemporary case, and, thus, was posed only to the two biblical cases.[45] In the Old and New Testament cases, the Ten Words are God's gracious accommodation to the participants, to expose the old and assist in learning the new. Learning the covenantal way of life was understood to be lifelong, difficult, and necessary. And, it was intended to be passed on to others, principally the next generation.

For over three thousand years, the Ten Words have had much the same pivotal role and function. Based on replication of parallel focus, need, differentiation between covenantal way of life and other worldviews, role of the Ten Words, and extent of their use across three case studies in three different eras, cultures and languages, their role and use has been to induct new members in covenantal living, effectively answering the main research question. They focus New Covenant believers on God and his great power on their behalf, teach what God is like and not like and what his reality implies for daily life, test believer's resolve and trust in God, create hope of a new way of life, teach principally to

---

45 The scope of the contemporary case study excluded the possibility of measuring or rating the extent to which the Ten Words/Covenant was used to instruct unchurched participants.

love God appropriately to who he is and our fellow man, and to pass this on to others, principally our children.

Jesus instructed his disciples before leaving that their principal task was to make disciples from all peoples, baptize them, and teach them all that Jesus had instructed them. The Ten Words form the core of what the church needs to fully instruct members of the covenant community in living a covenantal way of life and engaging the worldviews around them. Their critical power and authority and relevance to all aspects of life reflect a full-orbed understanding of the Covenant.

What are the implications of these findings and theory? It is for others to attempt to replicate, test and expand upon them. Some will certainly attempt to disprove such findings as that the same teaching could have universal, or at least sweeping, relevance over a span of time and cultures.

Calvin, the reputed father of covenantal theology, observed that conversion was necessary to the covenantal life. Worldview transformation or conversion was delimited from this present study. It is hoped that this will be remedied quickly. In addition, it would be instructive to measure to what extent unchurched Americans have received Ten Word/covenant instruction, and in what condition (directly, from previous generations who were churched, and so forth). Further recommendations for testing the usability of worldview for the covenantal understanding of life and reality were proffered at the end of chapters six and seven.

APPENDIX 1

RESEARCH DESIGN PROTOCOL

1. *Design*
   a. Determine and define *research questions*
   b. Select the *case(s)*/identify population(s)
   c. Determine data gathering and analysis *techniques*
   d. Determine, craft, and test *protocol* itself

2. *Qualitative Interview*
   a. Craft and test instrument(s)
   b. "Interview" ancient text *transcripts*
   c. Apply *questionnaire* to contemporary respondents

3. Conduct case study
   a. Prepare and collect data
   b. Protect *chain of evidence*
   c. Using *concept mapping, tack iteratively* between design, collection, analyses, & literature (theory)

4. Analyze and *triangulate*
   a. Analyze utilizing *qualitative & quantitative* methods
   b. Conduct *within-case* analyses
   c. Compare *cross-case replication* with other cases
   d. Consult literature (*theory*)

5. Reach *closure*: develop conclusions, recommendations, and implications based on findings:
   a. Summarize findings
   b. Derive conclusions & formulate *theory*
   c. Explore implications, including replication
   d. Make recommendations

6. Prepare/write the report

APPENDIX 2

CASE THREE INSTRUMENT PROTOCOL

1. Conduct exegesis of Exo 20 and Deu 5; research key words in these texts using other sources, such as TDOT.

2. Conduct content search throughout Scripture to locate versions of the Ten Words.

3. Conduct exegesis of Eph 4-5 and key word research using other sources such as NIDOTTE.

4. Write Old and New Testament Case Studies.

5. Develop one common research question for all three case studies: "By what means and to what extent were the Ten Words (Commandments) used to disciple the nations into the covenantal way of life, or to become functioning members of the covenant community?," with five subsidiary questions, listed above.

6. On the basis of five substantial repeats/versions of the Ten Words in Scripture, discover the issue involved for each of the Ten Words.

7. Develop ten categories of life/topics based on the ten issues.

8. Review instrument/questionnaire with select key informants in three sets: Christian: reformed and broadly evangelical; profession: academic/researchers, other business and professional, and a housewife; gender: male and female.

9. Develop instrument based on these topics and content: (test personal interview, hard-copy self-test, online self-test—Google.doc); select Google.doc format (results appear on downloadable spreadsheet).

10. Test Google.doc format of ten questions; adjust question wording and topics; rearrange in random order of questions:

                10 Word Order | Question Order
                     1   =   3
                     2   =   1
                     3   =   5
                     4   =   7

5	=	4
6	=	10
7	=	9
8	=	6
9	=	2
10	=	8

Testing Procedure Protocol:

11. Develop protocols for three groups: Group One (Unchurched), Group Two (Newly (re)churched, Group Three (Churched); group two failed to respond, so three becomes two. Recruit two groups of responders of five to eight each; Group One (Unchurched: 5 respondents); Group Two (third) (Churched: (8 respondents).

12. Conduct online testing (see protocols) during two week period in January 2009.

Treatment of Data:

13. Download spreadsheet and convert to straight text, one document per group; see "Transcript: Group One (Unchurched)" in Appendix.

14. Create text summaries: one page summary per respondent by response; summary by question of each group; see "Worldview Self-test Comparison Group One, by Respondent, #5" in Appendix.

15. Rasch-type analysis: tabulate response summaries along a Likert-type scale of 1-5, assigning numerical values to five descriptors:

   1: Learning directly attributable to source other than/opposite to the Ten Words/Bible

   2: Influenced by source other than the Bible

   3: Mixed or partly congruent with Ten Words/unclear source

   4: Influenced by scriptural teaching, possibly Ten Words

   5: Alike: respondent cited actual command or similar scriptural teaching or described using other words. See "Ten Words Comparison With Group One, Respondent #1" in Appendix.

Findings

16. Summarize Transcript.

17. Chart scores for each question and by each respondent for each group; using these charts, compare respondents within a group by question, and across both groups; compare questions within a group by respondent; compare group averages; compare combined scores for both groups, and across groups. See "Ten Words Comparison With Group One Summary" in Appendix.

18. Develop simple statistical analysis of both groups and contrast the two results.

19. Evaluate responses covenantally compared to fixed/external criteria (Ten Words/issues) as a whole and by group.

20. Summarize findings

APPENDIX 3

GROUP ONE TEST PROTOCOL

L.B. suggested that I talk with you.

I am in the research and writing stage of a study of worldview. My general topic area is the role of the Ten Commandments in discipling the nations (Mat 28:18-20). I am doing two biblical case studies (Moses and Paul) to show how they used the Ten Commandments to help new believers become functioning members of the covenant community. I also plan to survey three church populations to investigate how that is occurring today. The three populations I have in mind are: (1) unchurched who recently have begun attending church; (2) those from group one that have become church members a year or less ago; (3) long-term church members (more than 10 years).

So, here is my request: Can you introduce me to the unchurched people within your circle? I need to randomly select (3-5) individuals to conduct self-tests of their worldview.

What do you think? Is this feasible? I would appreciate it if you would help me by opening some doors.

Thanks for considering, and I look forward to talking with you soon.

Protocol: "D1" = Group 1 Unchurched (Dave) (Jan 6 http://spreadsheets. google. com/viewform?key= pB05LTp74bVOLJ1R4K0R4dQ)

Group #1
1. Ask permission
2. Make announcement and gather volunteers' names and emails
3. Make list
4. Send Intro emails
5. Gather Test results and tabulate

Sent	Name	E-Mail	Introduced	By
x	B.C.		D.E.	1
x	G.B.		D.E.	2
x	S.L.		D.E.	x6x
x	D.S.		D.E.	3
x	D.T.		D.E.	x7xx
x	M.F.		D.E.	4
x	B.C.		W.	5
x	T.D.		W.	x8 xx

Cells:
Gender: M-6, F-2

Email #1:
Thank you for being willing to take the Worldview Self-Test.
Please, reply immediately to confirm that I have correctly entered your email address.

THANKS!

Email #2:
Thank you for your willingness to help.

The purpose of this questionnaire is to research people's self-understanding of their worldview. The anonymous findings will be published in a research dissertation.

I hope that it may be insightful for you as well. The test is a simple-to-use online instrument. It could take anywhere from 10-30 minutes, depending on the person.

There are no right or wrong answers; answer what is valid for you. The lighter wording is intended as helper questions--you do not need to answer all of them. You may think that the wording betrays a particular bias, but you may treat the questions according to yours.

Write your first thoughts, not a book! Try to limit yourself to 3-4 minutes or 1-2 short paragraphs per question.

You may not be used to some of the language, or thinking about things this way. That is okay. To help understand a question, think of the main topic of the particular question and what is being asked about it. If you get stuck, just go on to the next question.

If you wish to discuss further, or desire a summary of the findings, please contact me at: db@porter.net

Deadline: January 18, 2009   THANK you for your help! Dan Porter

I've invited you to fill out the form "Worldview Self-Test". To fill it out, visit:
http://spreadsheets.google.com/viewform ?key=pB05LTp74bVNhxHwVohQudQ

Again, thanks,

Receive online results

5. Analysis:

a. Discard incompletes, rogue/extremes, or, in the case of too many respondents, a random group

b. Group answers and display on a Likert scale of 1-10

c. Summarize by group

d. Ask SQs of these

6. Followup:

Email #3:

Thank you for participating in the online Worldview Self-test prototype. If you have feedback please do not hesitate to let me know re:

-the whole process (being asked, pre-emails, online test, post- communication, etc.)

-the online experience of using the URL

-the instrument itself--difficulty, clarity or anything else regarding the questions

-anything else you would like to communicate

If you would like a summary of the final report, please let me know.

APPENDIX 4

Worldview Self-Test

The purpose of this questionnaire is to research people's self-understanding of their worldview. The anonymous findings will be published in a research dissertation.

There are no right or wrong answers; answer what is valid for you. The smaller wording is intended as helper questions--you do not need to answer all of them. You may think that the wording betrays a particular bias, but you may treat them according to yours.

Write your first thoughts, not a book! Try to limit yourself to 3-4 minutes, or 1-2 short paragraphs, per question.

You may not be used to some of the language, or thinking about things this way. That is okay. To help understand a question, think of the main topic of the particular question, and what is being asked about it. If you get stuck, just go on to the next question.

If you wish to discuss further, or desire a summary of the findings, please contact me at: db@porter.net.

Deadline: January 18, 2009   THANK you for your help!

* Required

Informed Consent *
I acknowledge that I have been informed of, and understand, the nature and purpose of this study, and I freely consent to participate. I understand that the information that I provide is entirely anonymous. (Please, enter "Yes")

1. The nature of Reality:
How do you understand reality? (Include the imaginary, if you wish) What is really real? Do you believe in an Ultimate reality? How do you know?

2. Integrity:
How are justice, truth, trust, honesty vs lying, cheating and deceit perceived, demonstrated in your life?

3. What you Value:
What or who is the most important thing in life, the highest value to you? To what or to whom do you give allegiance? Rank some of your values.

4. Trust and Respect:

Whom do you respect; trust? Or, on what do you base these? What/who is the basis for your authority? How do you honor/respect authority? Or, to what extent and on what basis would you honor/respect someone or an institution?

5. Power and Influence:

How do you view and use power/authority? Or, how do you think it should be used or not, and for what ends?

6. Value of the Individual and His Work:

What are your attitudes towards the value of the individual; work; personal property? What are your attitudes regarding theft, corruption, waste, redistribution of wealth?

7. A Question of Limits:

How do you understand boundaries or limits? Or, do you believe in limits? What is your attitude towards keeping things in proportion or not?

8. Pleasure and Appetite:

What do you covet, desire, envy, long for? How do you (attempt to) acquire: prestige, power, wealth, things?

9. Loyalty and Lust:

How do you feel about marriage, adultery, pornography; other expressions of loyalty or its opposite? Do you view loyalty and lust as mutually exclusive?

10. Life and Death:

How would you explain your position on life and death? What value do you place on life? What are your attitudes toward life? How should it be lived? How should it end? Is there anything after it?

Questions? Or discussion?   Be sure to include contact info (Optional)
Powered by Google Docs

APPENDIX 5

TRANSCRIPT: GROUP ONE (UNCHURCHED)

1. *The Nature of Reality*:
1. Reality to me is the belief what what I experience or perceive to exist. You don't necessarily need to touch it to be real. What is really real? For every person it's different because it includes emotions, belief and perceptions. What's real to me for example my anger over something may not be real to someone else. as for an Ultimate Reality - if you define that as God or the holy spirit then yes. How do I know... again it's based on my experiences and beliefs that it exists.

2. Yes, I believe in an "ultimate" reality. I believe in a scientific view of reality, and by definition there is only one truth. However, I also believe that perception of reality can be radically different based on your perspective, a la Einstein's theory of relativity. I'm not sure humans can perceive all of reality though.

3. Reality is what I see, smell, taste, hear and touch using all my senses at once if necessary. What is really real is really real. I don't know what an "ultimate reality" is except for death, taxes and the end of the month close.

4. What is the definition of reality? What I see in front of me or the understanding of the reality of the universe? Is this a physical perspective or a religious perspective? I don't believe from the physical world what I cannot verify. From a religious perspective I believe what I have not seen.

5. I think that God the Father is the Ultimate reality. I think that what is really real is the unseen, spiritual realm. I think that physical "reality", or existence, is a part of the whole, but I do not think that it is the complete whole or even half of the whole. I think that physical reality is like a dream we have at night, when sleeping. We think physical reality is "all there is" because we are creatures of our sight, hearing, smell, touch, etc. with a flesh, bone and blood body. But I believe that the unseen is more real than all of what we know through our physical senses.

2. *Integrity*:
1. The "vs" takes place every day.... it's the ongoing battle of good and evil. Because I have definition each of these categories... every day I'm faced with issues that either go against my perceived values or support the values. Usually through conversation you can uncover where it stands. For example if my husband says he'll be home by 9PM but doesn't arrive until 1AM without a call... at first i worry about is he safe. then my mind goes to he wasn't honest with me... then it goes thru what's he doing? But if at 8:30 he calls and says i know i was to

be home at 9PM but I'm having too much fun and want to stay until Midnight... then he's being honest and we can truthfully talk about if I'm comfortable.

2. Integrity is what holds society together so it adds value. And as socialized creatures we value and desire to have integrity, just like a dog wants to please a person. And because other people value Integrity, over the long-term people with Integrity are rewarded by better social success. I do believe this is "built in" to people, genetically not just learned.

3. I believe in justice, truthfulness and honesty and live that way. My friends/family would say that I show such traits. I don't like people who do not act with such traits. Sometimes regarding truth and honesty, I use "errors of omission" rather than "errors of commission" if this helps the situation.

4. These decisions are made moment to moment that I should not comprimise who I want to be and how I want to be perceived. It is demonstrated in my life by not making the easy choices but the wise choices.

5. I measure my own honesty by how I act when no one is watching me. The older I become, the more I try to be the best person that I can be. I want my life's fruit to be truth and honesty. I do not treat people unfairly. I do not cheat anyone, regardless of how young, or old, rich or poor that they may be. I strive to treat people the way that I want them to treat me - that's a good rule-of-thumb to follow. I do not always tell the truth, but it's usually to spare some one's feelings and usually a small or superficial thing, most often based on their appearance or something that would lower their spirits or confidence if I told them the "brutal truth". But if it was something that is beyond that, I would be as tactfully honest as I can be. I feel that I'm pretty good in the integrity department - probably better than most folks.

3. *What you Value*:
1. God is the highest...followed by: Family Friends Work/making a living to support a lifestyle Contributing to society for the positive Animals Working out/bettering myself Allegiance is something interesting. I pledge the allegiance to the USA... but I also align my self with God and Jesus as well as my family. Again it goes in ranking of above.

2. 1. Immediate family (wife & children) 2. Friends 3. Extended family 4. Work associates.

3. MOst important things in my life in rank order: The 4 "F's" plus "H" -- Family, Faith, Health, Friends, Financial position. I give allegiance to all of these.

4. What I have to put as the most important thing in my life is God and I'm rarely good at doing that. God would be my first allegiance (and I have to do better at that), my wife, my family, and then my job. Everything else falls pretty distant after that.

5. God The Father and Jesus The Christ. I do not give blind political alegience to anyone - especially an idiot like George Bush.

4. *Trust and Respect*:

1. My family and friends are obviously at the top. Respect and Trust is earned not given -- all through action and alignment of beliefs. Although there are people that i respect who don't share the exact beliefs. Not certain of the authority portion --- need to ponder further.

2. Trust and respect are VERY different. I respect many people I don't trust, and vice versa. I respect skills, knowledge, and work ethic. I trust based on track record of keeping promises and honesty. Both must be proven by direct or indirect actions. Indirect actions are awards or recommendations from trusted assiciates. Ultimately I respect people who can teach me something that will make me better. I trust people whom I can open up with and expose my weaknesses or rely on. I don't particularly honor/respect institutions.

3. I respect and trust those who earn it. I start with respect for most persons and adjust based on experience from there. The basis of my authority is what God gives me such as head of the family or manager in business. I respect authority of those who are capable.

4. I trust my wife. After that trust is earned. I am not sure what is meant by the 'basis of my authority'. Authority can be organizational, relational, and probably some other ways I can't think of immediately. If you ask how I show respect it can vary: showing agreement publicly, displaying disagreement privately, and doing what I commit (among others). I can't think of an institution that I respect. I respect individuals who stand by their committments and show their respect to others as well.

5. I respect and trust people who strive to do the right thing. They don't always have to be successful, but they have to want to be and they have to try. I trust people that I perceive are able to police themselves, who want to do the right thing even when no one is watching them - especially when no one is watching them. This is how I police myself. An institution is more difficult to trust because it is made up of many different people with many different thought forms and beliefs of what is right and what is wrong. People can look honest and talk-the-talk, yet still be crooked as a snake. I trust a person or an institution based on the reasults - the fruit - of what they do.I base these beliefs on the Bible and my

upbringing in the church. Jesus is the example I try to follow. The question "What would Jesus do?" is a good rule of thumb to go by.

5. *Power and Influence*:
1. Power and authority should be used as guidelines to keep order in society. It should not be abused... it should be enforced and checks and balances put in place to ensure no corruption takes place.

2. Power is usually earned, I've met very few powerfull people who didn't deserve it at some point in their lives. However, once it is earned, it can be given (ie, control of money). Power should be used benevelevently, because it will be taken away if it isn't. Yes, those with power have a responsibility to use it.

3. Power and authority are necessary whenever there are groups or masses to insure order. Without order there is chaos. Of course, such power should be used to help the whole group rather than just the individuals.

4. I view authority as something that can be used to lead people or accomplish goals. Authority should be used to do the wise thing.

5. Just like with anything - fire for instance - power and authority can be used for good or ill purposes. It has to be used, but for the highest and best causes. Fire can warm or kill, depending on the motivations behind the wielder of its use. I use power to accomplish my personal goals. I try to use my authority to accomplish what I percieve as good. But I am also aware that what I think is good, others may not agree with. It's all realitive.

6. *Value of the Individual and his Work*:
1. In today's society - I believe that you work to make a positive impact and contribute above what's required to you.   As for personal property... it's material.. .while I like "things" theres even greater pleasure to me in giving. Theft, corruption, waste... drives me nuts... believe we don't have accountability in our society or repercussions any longer.   People should be punished for wrong doings. As for redistribution of wealth.   I believe we should help that people that need help... but that's not giving them our money... that's providing the basics.

2. I'm a strong free-market capitalist, and have a strong protestant work ethic. Individuals have value in what they can contribute to society, but the "invisible hand of the market" causes selfish behaviours to improve the whole. I'm opposed to redistribution of wealth unless by market forces (which it will ineviably do). The only hitch with this is that transparency is needed to prevent corruption and theft causing the system to fail.

3. Work is God's way to let one use the personal attributes that God has given each person. If u do not use such talents, you are often not happy. I have had a few periods in my life where I did not work. I was happy for a brief while, but unhappy until I went back to work using my talents. I believe those who do not work or have a good work ethic are missing out on one of the great feelings in life - the good feeling one gets whe one is contributing and being successful. Theft/corruption - hate these. Waste - dont like but happens. Redistribution of wealth - ok a little bit, but not to those who chose not to work.

4. From a political standpoint everything is about the individual. I do not believe in the redistribution of wealth as that leads to the degredation of society. Those who have their needs handed to them have no need to contribute to the development of society. Our society was built on the lives of individuals who did not hesitate to give all they had to protect teh constitution. Today, it's more about what others can do for the individual than what the individual can do for themselves.

5. I feel very strongly about people working for what they want. The attitude of entitlement is something that really bothers me.It's probably easier for me to say these things because I have known very little true want in my life. Nevertheless, I look down on theft, corruption an waste. I do not believe in the "redistribution" of wealth. I work hard for what I have and do not feel that someone else is "entitled" to a portion of it, when they are lazy and do not want to work as hard as I do. I do believe in tithing a portion of what I make to the church, charitable causes or the needy. But I like it to be my choice. I do not like the idea of a wasteful beuriocacy taking a portion to goes to support lazy, slothful people that want to get high and take without contributing to the betterment of society. That type of person makes be boiling mad. There was a recent documentary about a social experiment, where a homeless man was given $100K. The long and short of it was that he was broke again within less than 2 years. He said that the money turned out to be a burden for him. He did not know how to use it properly and keeping up with all the payments, rent, upkeep, etc. was awful to him. Unless we are taught good stewardship, we will waste our opportunities. I value my personal property and do not allow access to it by anyone that I feel is sloppy, lazy or not likely to respect my stuff as much as I do.I feel that my "stuff" is the fruit of my good labor.

7. *A Question of Limits*:
1. Boundry are based on the 10 commandments but then also the laws of the countries. I also place limits on myself to keep my beliefs in check. as for keeping things in propotion - it would depend on the item.

2. Limits and boundaries are flexible depending on the situation. I don't generally believe in hard rules. Keeping things in proportion is important, but those who don't will fail anyway.

3. BOundaries and limits are necessary in organizations/countries to have order. Limits and boundaries are good for people as well except when one's freedom, creativity or success are artificial limited. I believe in the law of equilibrium in that everything in life works around each person's equilibrium. THings in all aspects of life go up and down around each one's equilibrium chart and we need to keep this in perspective.

4. I do believe in boundaries to the individual. Boundaries are given by other individuals and respected by those to whom they are given. There are boundaries imposed by individuals, by laws, and by social mores. I am not sure how keeping things in proportion are related to boundaries.

5. I understand boundries as a line that you don't cross. It could be for your own protection or that of another. I do believe in limits for creatures of the physical world - we seem to need them. I think that in the unseen side of life, there are very few limits, but I don't know what they necessarily are. God himself has mandated them form his other creatures on the side that is invisible to us. I like to keep things in proportion. Too much of even a good thing is still "too much". I also believe that boundries are a guideline - not an absolute, every single time. Sometimes rules have to be broken for the sake of justice or mercy. Inflexibility is not good.

8. *Pleasure and Appetite*:
1. To serve people gives me the greatest pleasure... i prefer to be in the background doing little things that make a big difference in the life. I do attempt to gain weath but it's to be able to ongoingly give.

2. Maslow's heirarchy of needs: food, shelter, security, love, self-actualization. Pretty straightforward. I'm at the security step right now. Want to get to the point where I don't worry about money. Power is important to my ego, but I'm learning as I get older (I'm 37) that it really isn't needed.

3. I covet financial security, family happiness and inner peace. I acquire prestige and power via success at work and in organizations. I acquire wealth via work and investments.

4. I long for kids that grow to be responsible adults and good parents. I have found it easier not to covet or envy as I get older as that is wasted energy and doesn't help to accomplish any goals. I believe in acquiring wealth but not at the expense of comprimising my morals. I had the opportunities for great wealth and lost my chance of that because of greed.

5. I don't think that I really covet anything that another has. There are things that I see that I would also like to have, but I don't think that is the same thing as

coveting it. The closest I may come to that is my longing for a good mate and a secure home environment - my mate and home, not the mate or home of someone else. I desire and long for things, but not to the point of covetousness or envy; it's more like wistfulness.I do think that it is The Father's will that I be happy and satisfied in these areas, so I believe that I too, shall be satisfied in these areas - without having to steal my satisfaction from another. How do I attempt to acquire prestige, power and things? That is a very good question! I feel that I take my power and prestige by living what I believe those things to be.I think that people attribute those things to others when they see people living ethically and conducting themselves with honor. To acquire wealth, I go to work and do my best to earn the things that I wish to have, like nice clothes,and jewelry. I love cooking and eating beautiful and delicious food, but I don't stuff in crap, just to feel full. I think about the quality of my fullness. I also think that being grateful for what I do have and being generous to the best of my ability is what prompts the universe to supply my wants and needs. I truly believe that when I pinch off giving to others, my receiving gets pinched off in direct proportion. That is a lesson I am very focused about working on at this point in my life. I feel good about my progress. The more I give, the more I seem to be getting.

9. *Loyalty or Lust*:
1. Believe in the institution of marriage and the loyalty and exclusiveness of the "agreement". loyalty and lust are not at all the same. You can be loyal to a male friend and have no lust involved.

2. Hmmm. Not mutually exclusive. Lust is just an emotion that doesn't matter without actions. Porn is not adultery. Marriage is the ulimate committment of loyalty. However, adultery and temporary indescressions are not a reasons to end marriages. If my wife had an affair, I hope she would never tell me. I worry much more about emotional affairs and sexual.

3. Marriage - great with the right person. Adultery - fun for a while, but bad in the long term. Pornography - interesting to look at, but bad for your being. Loyalty and lust do not need to be mutually exclusive. You can "window shop" without buying if you catch my drift.

4.I believe in the sanctity of marriage and loyalty to it. I also understand the temptations in the world and the ease that they can be accessed. Do I view loyalty and lust as mutually exclusive? I think loyalty is a long term committment and lust is a short term fall. They can exist mutually in the short term but not the long term.

5. I believe in marriage. I believe that it can be man and woman's sweetest form of existence to have a beloved mate to go through and share life with. I know that it can also be Hell on Earth to be hooked into living with a person that is not a

good match. I think that adultry is is one of the worst forms of betrayal, but I also know that many people are driven to adultry by either a poor mate selection or immaturity and failure to attain adult sympathy, understanding and love (selfishness). It is a bit too simplistic to say that loyalty and lust are mutually exclusive. I think that many people - of both sexes - have felt "forbidden" lust, especially when they are not satisfied at home. But I also believe that this dissatisfaction may be the fault of the immature, selfish person who has failed to gain an adult understanding of life and the world. I believe that pornography can be fascinating to watch, for the spiritually and emotionally healthy individual, but can be very destructive for a person that is unsatisfied and has "issues" going on in their life. In order to continue physical procreation, I believe that God have give us powerful hormones that "drive" us towards the pleasures of the flesh. Physical comfort and connection are paramount to me, too. Infants and young children will die or develop improperly from lack of physical touch and connection. Humans are hard-wired to need this. There is no black or white answer to the question of "loyalty vs. lust".But I do believe that a properly developed (spiritually) person will find the satisfaction of their lust within the loyalty of a happily mated pair-bond.

10. *Life and Death*:
1. I belive that there is life after death however life has huge value and another person does not have the right to take it. Life should be lived in accordance to the laws of the bible - but you should live life to the fullest. How should it end? No one knows how anyones life should end... ideally peacefully and not at the hands of some else or by your own hand. Yes there is definely life after death.

2. I'm a clear agnostic, kinda believe in god but not sure I believe in an afterlife. If Hell is the absence of God, then maybe Hell is really that last fleeting second, feeling bad about how you've lieved your life. Don't want that either. So I'm undecided.

3. Life is a journey that has ups and downs and revolves around each person's God given talents and equilibrium. Death is not fun, but is inevitable. I have noticed over the years that many people who die in old age chose to do so at some point as they no longer want to live for various reasons. Life is very valuable. With that said, I do believe in abortion as I think it is worse to bring someone into that world that is not wanted or has serious disabilities. Life should be lived with balance between what is important to each person without hurting others. Heaven can wait.

4. Life is and death will be. Live your life to the best that you can and there will be no regrets at death. I place great value on the lives of individuals except for those who have no respect for it themselves. How SHOULD life end? I don't really know, I don't really think about it. I've seen my mother die from cancer and

wouldn't want to die that way, but I never really think about how it should end. And yes, there is something after it. I believe in Jesus Christ and Heaven as much as I know there is evil in the world and a Hell afterwards. The question always becomes why are we here? The problem is that people don't want to believe in a higher power and that we are here to serve him.

5. I place a great value on life. I do not, however, give the unborn rights over the all ready born. I feel strongly that humans need to have passed through the womb and survived on this side of life before their "Constitutional rights" kick in. It makes me crazy at the thought of sacrificing the life of a LIVING mother in favor of an UNBORN child, unless the mother will for sure die but the child might have a chance to live (car accident, coma, etc.). I also believe in the right of the terminally ill to mercifully end their life, if that is what they wish. I do not believe that God will damn the human soul of someone who is suffering physically, mentally or emotionally, if they take their own life. Some times some souls just need to go back home. God has given me a body, and a soul and free-will to run them both. Free-will automatically implies that I have the "right" to make "wrong" choices, either intentionally or out of ignorance. I believe that we are here on Earth to learn how to choose the will of the Father over our own. But I also believe that we have a right to not learn from our mistakes if that is what we choose. I believe that "the affectionate dedication of the human will to the doing of the Father's will is man's choicest gift to God". (The Urantia Book, pg.22, par.5) I want to live my life in the ever evolving process of trying to discover what his will for me is, whether through reading of The Bible, reading of other books, and learning other peoples thoughts, as well as the wisdom gleaned from my own personal life experience. My hope is that my life will end sweetly, while I sleep in my bed. I believe that Jesus will send his holy angels to fetch me and bring me directly into his presence. I also believe that he allows the loved ones who have proceeded me to be part of the "welcoming committee". That is one of my greatest joys - the thought of my loved ones welcoming me into the eternal home that he has prepared for all of us.

APPENDIX 6

WORLDVIEW SELF-TEST COMPARISON, GROUP TWO, RESPONDENT #5

1. The Nature of Reality: Real, true, not imagination or desire

2. Integrity: Lying, etc. = sin; justice and truth = virtues

3. What you value: Christ, family, church, friends

4. Trust and Respect: Respect: family, church leaders, friends; authority figures = deserve if demonstrated; highly respect older = demonstrated wisdom; respect: experience and discernment

5. Power and Influence: God given & accountability; used wisely for safety and improve humans

6. Value of the Individual and his Work: Each precious to God; Creator gives work to develop and use us for his glory; personal property = 1 of God's blessings; theft, etc. = greed

7. A Question of Limits: = Important, to use time wisely and not wear out; = important to keep proportion and balance

8. Pleasure and Appetite: Covet: deep walk with the Lord, accept Lord's gifts; no desire: acquire other than what Lord sees fit to give

9. Loyalty or Lust: Marriage = God given; = total opposites; adultery/porno = sin of lust

10. Life and Death: God gives life; = precious, value; death = end of earthly life, = release soul to eternal kingdom, enjoy God forever; should live for God's glory seeking to obey and please him in everything

APPENDIX 7

TEN WORDS COMPARISON WITH GROUP ONE, RESPONDENT #5

CATEGORY-ISSUE	AMERICAN UNCHURCHED WORLDVIEW	LIKERT SCALE 1-5
1. What/Who you Value 1 God only, distinct from man	God; no blind allegiance to any man (like idiot GWB)	(similar) 4
2. Nature of Reality Non-negotiable acceptble worship	UR=God/Father; unseen realm; physical only part, a dream (Eastern mystic)	1 (opposite)
3. Power & Influence Lord's reputation/ way; right use of power	Should: use for good, for highest & best causes, accomplish personal goals; for good/ill; all=relative; disagree what is good	3 (partly true)
4. Question of Limits Grace, not merit, gives propor-tion/boundaries	= uncrossable line, for own/ others' protection; like to keep proportion; = guidelines, not inflexible; sometimes must break for mercy/justice sake; God mandates few limits in unseen world	4
5. Trust & Respect Honor/respect authority based on Father/family	Should strive to; respect those who want & try, ≠ successful; trust those who police selves like I do, not prima facie, father/family but fruit basis: Bible, upbringing, WWJD	2 (distant)
6. Life and Death Respect human life & otherness	Believe; place great value on life; OK: abortion & assisted suicide; purpose: discover God's will & do; hope: angels bring me to heaven & loved ones welcome me	1

CATEGORY-ISSUE	AMERICAN UNCHURCHED WORLDVIEW	LIKERT SCALE 1-5
7. Loyalty or Lust Love & loyalty/ integrity of family = criteria of relationships	=Marriage, sweetest form of existence OR hell on earth w/wrong person; loyalty & lust≠; mutually exclusive=too simplistic; OK: feel forbidden lust; can be driven to; adultery=worst betrayal; procreation requires powerful hormones to drive us to flesh; pleasure/satisfy lust within happy marriage loyalty	2
8. Value of Person & Work Value of person livelihood, including trespass & basis for redistribution	= contribute to societal betterment; work for what I want, = my fruit; no: redistribute wealth; need to teach good stewardship; best: tithe, voluntarily give, my choice, not bureaucratic taking; no: entitlement, theft takes; self-reliance (Self-reliant)	4
9. Integrity Truth vs deceit/inocu-lation destroys reputation, relation-ships	Measure=how I act alone; try/ strive to be best person I can; OK: shade small truths to spare feelings, not big truths; I'm pretty good	3
10. Pleasure and Appetite Purity not Eros-desire/heart idolatry, acquiring	Like to have things; long for things = wistful; happy & satisfied = God's will; don't covet; take power & prestige by living beliefs; acquire = work & effort; earn needs by effort at giving	4

APPENDIX 8

TEN WORDS COMPARISON WITH GROUP TWO SUMMARY

CATEGORY-ISSUE	AMERICAN CHURCHED WORLDVIEW	LIKERT SCALE 1-5
1. What/Who you Value 1 God only, distinct from man	1(3) = God (7/8) = family (6/8) = values (3/8)	4(35)
2. Nature of Reality Non-negotiable acceptble worship	2(1) = real, true, actual (3/8) = two realities? (4/8)	(28) 3
3. Power & Influence Lord's reputation/ way; right use of power	3(5) Criteria = God/Bible (4/8) = purpose/end (4/8) = the good (4/8)	(31) 4
4. Question of Limits Grace, not merit, gives proportion/ boundaries	4(7) = important, essential, necessary (5/8) + law (1/8) + safeguard (1/8) = (7/8)	(27) 3
5. Trust & Respect Honor/respect authority based on Father/family	5(4) Standard = Bible (5/8) = God ordained, authority (3/8) = earned (3/8)	(33)4
6. Life and Death Respect human life & otherness	6(10)= God (only, glorify, etc. (7/8) = Yes: afterlife (5/8)	(34)4

159

CATEGORY-ISSUE	AMERICAN CHURCHED WORLDVIEW	LIKERT SCALE 1-5
7. Loyalty or Lust Love & loyalty/ integrity of family = criteria of relationships	7(9) = Marriage (7/8) = God revealed/based (4/8) = mutually exclusive (4/8); not (1/8) = lust=sin (3/8) = avoid/fence (3/8)	4(36)
8. Value of Person & Work Value of person; livelihood, including trespass & basis for redistribution	8(6) God (7/8): values each (5/8); ordained, from (4/8) Redistribution = evil (3/8), disheartens (1/8)= (4/8) work->property (3/8) Theft, etc. = sin (3/8)	(32) 4
9. Integrity Truth vs deceit/ inoculation destroys reputation, relationships	9(2) = Strive for (5/8) = Based in God/Bible (3/8) = sin (3/8)	(29)3
10. Pleasure and Appetite Purity, not Eros- desire/heart idolatry, acquiring	10(8)= comfort/ease (3/8); wealth (3/8) Admit covet (6/8); battle (1/8); no desire (1/8) Material (5/8); Spiritual (2/8)	(29)3

BIBLIOGRAPHY

Works Cited

Averbeck, Richard E. 1995. Law. Quoted in *Cracking Old Testament codes: A guide to interpreting Old Testament literary forms,* ed. D. Brent Sandy and Ronald L. Giese, Jr., 116-118, 121, 129, 134. Nashville: Broadman and Holman Publishers.

Baltzer, K. 1971. *The covenant formulary in Old Testament, Jewish, and early Christian writings.* Trans. D. E. Green. Philadelphia: Fortress Press. Quoted in *Cracking Old Testament codes: A guide to interpreting Old Testament literary forms,* ed. D. Brent Sandy and Ronald L. Giese, Jr., 118. Nashville: Broadman and Holman Publishers.

Barclay, William. 1973. *The Ten Commandments for today.* San Francisco: Harper and Row.

Barrs, Jerram. 1982. Christianity true to the way things are. Quoted in *What in the world is real?: Challenging the superficial in today's world.* Champagne, IL: Communication Institute.

Barth, Karl. 1960. *Church dogmatics.* Vol. 3. Ed. G. W. Bromiley and T. F. Torrance. Trans. G. W. Bromiley and R. J. Ehrlich. Edinburgh: T. & T. Clark. Quoted in David K. Naugle. *The history of a concept,* 335. Grand Rapids: Wm. B. Eerdmans Publishing Co., 2002.

Barth, Markus. 1974. *Ephesians.* NY: Doubleday. Quoted in D. A. Carson, Douglas J. Moo, and Leon Morris. *An introduction to the New Testament,* 309. Grand Rapids: Zondervan Publishing House, 1992.

Battles, Ford Lewis. 1977. God was accommodating himself to human capacity. *Interpretation* 31:19-38. Quoted in Donald K. McKim, ed. *Readings in Calvin's theology.* Grand Rapids: Baker, 1984. Quoted in Laurence C. Jr. Sibley. Baptizing the Nations: Mission, Culture and Liturgy in the Gospel of Matthew, 7. Research/writing project for 2003 Luce Seminar, Prospects of Historic Liturgies in a Postmodern Age. Philadelphia: Westminster Theological Seminary, 2004.

Bavinck, J. H. 1981. *The church between temple and mosque.* Reprint. Grand Rapids: William B. Eerdmans Publishing Company.

Bellah, Robert N., Richard Madsen, William M. Sullivan, Ann Swidler, and Steven M. Tipton. 1986. *Habits of the heart: Individualism and commitment in American life*. New York: Perennial Library.

Blake, Everett C., and Anna G. Edmonds. 2002. *Biblical sites in Turkey*. London: Milet, Ltd.

Bockmuehl, Klaus. 1994. *The Christian way of living: An ethics of the Ten Commandments*. Vancouver: Regent College Bookstore.

Braaten, Carl E., and Christopher R. Seitz, eds. 2005. *I am the Lord your God: Christian reflections on the Ten Commandments*. Grand Rapids: William B. Eerdmans Publishing Company.

Bulato, Jaime. 1992. *Split-level living*. Manila: Ateneo de Manilo. Quoted in Paul G. Hiebert, R. Daniel Shaw, and Tite Tiénou. *Understanding folk religion: A Christian response to popular beliefs and* practices, 15, n. 1. Grand Rapids: Baker Books, 2003.

Caligula. Lex col. Genetivae Iuliae. In *Corpus instriptionum Latinarum*. 1. LXX; LXXI. Quoted in Jerome, Carcopino. *Daily life in ancient Rome: The people and the city at the height of the empire*, 200. Ed. Henry T. Rowell, Trans. E. O. Lorimer. New Haven: Yale University Press, 1992.

Calvin, John. [1559] 1960. *Institutes of the Christian religion*. Trans. Lewis Battles. Ed. John T. McNeill. Philadelphia: The Westminster Press.

Carcopino, Jerome. 1992. *Daily life in ancient Rome: The people and the city at the height of the empire*. Ed. Henry T. Rowell. Trans. E. O. Lorimer. New Haven: Yale University Press.

Carson, D. A., Douglas J. Moo, and Leon Morris. 1992. *An introduction to the New Testament*. Grand Rapids: Zondervan Publishing House.

Cassuto, Umberto. 1972 (1961). *A commentary on the Book of Genesis. Part I: From Adam to Noah, Genesis 1-18*. Trans. Israel Abrahams. Jerusalem: The Magnes Press.

_____. 1987. *A commentary on Exodus*. Trans. Israel Abrahams. Jerusalem: The Magnes Press.

Cicero. *Numerous works of letters, speeches and philosophy, ad Att.; ad fam*. Quoted in T. P. Wiseman, ed. Competition and co-operation. *Roman political life 90 B.C. to A.D. 69*, 9. Exeter studies in history, no. 7, ed. Colin James. Exeter University Publication, 1985.

Clowney, Edmund P., and Rebecca Clowney Jones. 2007. *How Jesus transforms the Ten Commandments*. Phillipsburg, NJ: P & R Publishing.

Collison, J. G. F. 1985. Mission, the Word, and the Spirit. Paper presented at ATS Retreat. Quoted in Max Stackhouse. *Apologia: Contextualization, globalization, and mission in theological education*. Grand Rapids: William B. Eerdmans Publishing Company, 1988.

Corbett, Percy Ellwood. 1969. *The Roman law of marriage*. Oxford: Oxford University Press. Quoted in Jerome, Carcopino. *Daily life in ancient Rome: The people and the city at the height of the empire*, 94. Ed. Henry T. Rowell, Trans. E. O. Lorimer. New Haven: Yale University Press, 1992.

Creswell, John W. 1998. *Qualitative inquiry and research design*. Thousand Oaks, CA: SAGE Publications.

Cumont, Franz. 1911. *The oriental religions in Roman paganism*. Chicago: Open Court.

Currid, John D. 2001a. *A study commentary on Exodus*. Vol. 2. Evangelical study commentary. Auburn, MA: Evangelical Press.

_____. 2001b. OT508 Genesis-Deuteronomy Class Notes. Reformed Theological Seminary.

_____. 2007. The Hebrew world-and-life view. In *Revolutions in worldview: Understanding the flow of Western thought,* ed. W. Andrew Hoffecker. Phillipsburg, NJ: P&R Publishing.

Davidson, R. 1989. Covenant ideology in ancient Israel. In *The world of ancient Israel: Sociological, anthropological and political perspectives*, ed. R. E. Clements. Cambridge: Cambridge University Press. Quoted in D. Brent Sandy and Ronald L. Giese, Jr. *Cracking Old Testament codes: A guide to interpreting Old Testament literary* forms, 116. Nashville: Broadman and Holman Publishers, 1995.

Davies, Lloyd. 1997. Covenantal hermeneutics and the redemption of theory. *Christianity and Literature* 46, no. 3-4 (Spring): 357-397.

deSilva, David Arthur. 2000. *Honor, patronage, kinship and purity: Unlocking New Testament culture*. Downers Grove, IL: InterVarsity Press. Quoted in Gordon Fee. 2002. The cultural context of Ephesians 5:18-6:9. *Priscilla Papers* (Winter): 16:15-17. http://www.cbeinternational. org/new/pdf_files/free_articles/CulturalContext_Fee.pdf [accessed 12/08/2008].

Douma, J. 1992. *The Ten Commandments*. Trans. Nelson D. Kloosterman. Phillipsburg, NJ: P & R Publishing.

Dudley, Donald R. 1993. *The civilization of Rome*. NY: Meridian.

Eco, Umberto. 1976. *A theory of semiotics*. Advances in semiotics, ed. Thomas A. Sebeok. Bloomington: Indiana University Press. Quoted in David Naugle. *Worldview: The history of a concept*. Grand Rapids: William B. Eerdmans Publishing Company, 2002.

Edmondson, Stephen. 2005. Christ and history: Hermeneutical convergence in Calvin and its challenge to biblical theology. *Modern Theology* 21, no. 1 (January): 3-35.

Farley, Benjamin W. 1980. *John Calvin's sermons on the Ten Commandments*. Grand Rapids: Baker Books.

Feagin, J., A. Orum, and G. Sjoberg, eds. 1991. *A case for case study*. Chapel Hill, NC: University of North Carolina Press.

Fee, Gordon. 2002. The cultural context of Ephesians 5:18-6:9, *Priscilla Papers* (Winter): 16:15-17. http://www.cbe international.org/new/pdf_files/free_articles/Cultural Context_Fee.pdf [accessed 12/08/2008].

Fisch, Harold. 1988. *Poetry with a purpose: Biblical poetics and interpretation*. Bloomington, IL: Indiana University Press.

Fisch, Menachem. 1993. *Summoning: Ideas of the covenant and interpretive theory*. Ed. Ellen Spolsky. Albany: State U of New York Press. Quoted in Lloyd Davies. Covenantal hermeneutics and the redemption of theory. *Christianity and Literature* 46, no. 3-4 (Spring), 357-397, 1997.

Gangel, Kenneth. 2008. Teaching with case studies. http://www. bible.org/page.php?page_id= 2742 [accessed 06/23.2008].

Gräbe, Petrus J. 2006. *New covenant, new community: The significance of biblical and patristic covenant theology for current understanding* . Waynesboro, GA: Paternoster Press.

Haimowitz, Morris L., and Natalie Reader Haimowitz, eds. 1966. *Human development: Selected readings*, 2d ed. NY: Thomas Y. Crowell Company.

Hall, Edward T. 1959. *The silent language*. Greenwich, CT: Premier Fawcett.

Harland, Phillip A. 2003. *Associations, synagogues, and congregations: Claiming a place in ancient Mediterranean society*. Minneapolis: Fortress Press.

Harrison, R. K. 1970. *Introduction to the Old Testament*. London: The Tyndale Press.

Hiebert, Paul G. 1999. *Missiological implications of epistemological shifts: Affirming truth in a modern/postmodern world*. Harrisburg, PA: Trinity Press International.

Hiebert, Paul G., R. Daniel Shaw, and Tite Tiénou. 1999. *Understanding folk religion: A Christian response to popular beliefs and practices*. Grand Rapids: Baker Books.

Hirsch, Edward. 1967. *Validity in interpretation*. New Haven, CT: Yale University Press. In *Modern criticism and theory: A reader*. Ed. David Lodge and Nigel Wood. Harlow, England: Pearson.

_____. 2000. Introductory note, and faulty perspectives. In *Modern criticism and theory: A reader,* ed. David Lodge and Nigel Wood. Harlow, England: Pearson.

Hobbs, Rebecca, ed. 2000. How do you view the world? *Reformed Quarterly* 19, no. 1 (Spring). http://www.rts.edu/ quarterly/spring00/hoffecker [accessed 02/26/2009].

W. Andrew Hoffecker, ed. 1986. *Building a Christian world view*. Vol. 1. Phillipsburg, NJ: Presbyterian and Reformed Publishing Company.

Hoffecker, Andrew. 2007. *Revolutions in worldview: Understanding the flow of Western thought*. Phillipsburg, NJ: P&R Publishing.

_____. 2008. MS832 Worldview and worldview transformation lecture notes, including Covenant Law. Class handout. Jackson, MS: Reformed Theological Seminary.

Horton, Michael S. 2002. *Covenant and eschatology: The divine drama*. Louisville, KY: Westminster John Knox.

_____. 2006. *God of promise: Introducing covenant theology*. Grand Rapids: Baker Books.

Howard, V. A., and J. H. Barton. 1988. *Thinking on paper*. NY: Harper Perennial. Quoted in Joseph A. Maxwell. *Qualitative Research Design*. Qualitative Research Methods. Vol. 41, 36-42. Thousand Oaks, CA: Sage Publications, 1996.

Jones, Prudence, and Nigel Pennick. 1995. *A history of pagan Europe*. NY: Barnes and Noble Books.

Jones, W. T. 1972. World views: Their nature and their function. *Current anthropology* 13 (February):79-109. Quoted in David Naugle. *Worldview: The history of a concept*, 255. Grand Rapids: William B. Eerdmans Publishing Company, 2002.

Kaiser, Walter. 1987. *Toward rediscovering the Old Testament*. Grand Rapids: Zondervan Publishing.

Kearney, Michael. 1984. *World view*. Novato, CA: Chandler & Sharp.

Kimmerle, H. 1967. Hermeneutical theory or ontological hermeneutics. *Journal for theology and the church*: 107-21. Quoted in Anthony C. Thiselton. *The two horizons: New Testament hermeneutics and philosophical description*, 5. n. 6. Grand Rapids: William B. Eerdmans Publishing Company, 1980.

Kline, Meredith G. 1963. *The treaty of the great king: The covenant structure of Deuteronomy*. Grand Rapids: Eerdmans.

_____. 1968. *By oath consigned*. Grand Rapids: Zondervan Publishing.

Kreitzer, Mark R. 2006. *Intercultural ethics*. Self published.

Krystek, Lee. 1998. The temple of Artemis at Ephesus. http://www.unmuseum. org/ephesus/htm [accessed 11/26.2008].

Kuntz, Paul Grimley. 2004. *The Ten Commandments in history: Mosaic paradigms for a well-ordered society.* Ed. Thomas D'Evelyn. Grand Rapids: William B. Eerdmans.

Kuyper, Abraham. 1898. *Lectures on Calvinism.* Amsterdam: Hoocker and Wormser Ltd.

Larsen, Samuel H. 2006. Foundational christo-centric perspectives. Lecture notes. Jackson, MS: Reformed Theological Seminary.

_____. 2007. MS 861 Ethnographic research methods. Class notes. Jackson, MS: Reformed Theological Seminary.

_____. 2007. MS845 Intercultural Church Revitalization and Growth. Class notes. Jackson, MS: Reformed Theological Seminary.

_____. 2008. MS832 Worldview and worldview transformation. Lecture notes. Jackson, MS: Reformed Theological Seminary.

Leuchter, Mark. 2005. The temple sermon and the term in the Jeremianich corpus. *Journal for the Study of the Old Testament* 30, no. 1: 93-109.

Levi, Alda. 1936. *La patera d'argento di Parabiago.* Rome. Quoted in Jerome Carcopino. *Daily life in ancient Rome: The people and the city at the height of the empire*, 130. Ed. Henry T. Rowell, Trans. E.O. Lorimer. New Haven: Yale University Press, 1992.

Loisy. 1922. *Les myste;res paiens et le myste;re chrevtien.* Paris.

Loane, Helen J. 1983. *Industry and commerce of the city of Rome (50 B.C. - 200 A.D.).* Baltimore, MD: Johns Hopkins Press. Quoted in Jerome Carcopino. *Daily life in ancient Rome: The people and the city at the height of the empire*, 176. Ed. Henry T. Rowell, Trans. E.O. Lorimer. New Haven: Yale University Press, 1992.

Luther, Martin. 1962. To the councilmen of all cities in Germany that they establish and maintain Christian schools. In *The Christian in Society II.* Vol. 45 of *Luther's Works.* Ed. Walther I. Brandt. Transl. A.T.W. Steinhauser. Rev. W.I. Brandt. Philadelphia: Fortress Press. Quoted in David Naugle. *Worldview: The history of a concept*, 336. Grand Rapids: William B. Eerdmans Publishing Company, 2002.

Lyotard, Jean-François. 1984. *The postmodern condition: A report on knowledge.* Minneapolis: University of Minnesota Press. Quoted in David Naugle.

Worldview: The history of a concept, 257. Grand Rapids: William B. Eerdmans Publishing Company, 2002.

Maggiotto, Franco. 1997. Ten Words commentary. Torino: Fede Viva.

Maxwell, Joseph A. 1996. *Qualitative research design.* Qualitative Research Methods, vol. 41. Thousand Oaks, CA: Sage Publications.

McCarthy, D. J. 1981. Treaty and covenant. In *Analecta Biblica* 21A. Rev. ed. Rome: Biblical Institute Press.

Mendenhall, G. E. 1955. Law and covenant in Israel and the ancient Near East. *The Biblical Archaeologist* 17:26-76.

Metzger, Bruce M. 1994. *A textual commentary on the Greek New Testament.* 2d ed. NY: United Bible Societies.

Muller, Richard A. 1990. The hermeneutic of promise and fulfillment in Calvin's exegesis of the Old Testament prophecies of the kingdom. In *The Bible in the sixteenth century*, ed. David Steinmetz. Durham, NC: Duke University Press. Quoted in Stephen Edmondson. Christ and history: Hermeneutical convergence in Calvin and its challenge to biblical theology. *Modern Theology* 21, no. 1 (January) 3-35, 2005.

Frankfort-Nachmias, Chava, and David Nachmias. 1992. *Research methods in the social sciences.* 4th ed. London: Worth Publishing, Ltd. Quoted in Robert K. Yin. *Case study research: Design and methods*, 2d ed., 18. Newbury Park, CA: Sage, 1994.

Naugle, David. 2001. What is knowledge: Biblical/hebraic epistemology. Summer Institute in Christian Scholarship. lecture notes. Dallas Baptist University.

_____. 2002. *Worldview: The history of a concept*. Grand Rapids: William B. Eerdmans Publishing Company.

Ong, Walter. 1969. World as view and world as event. *American anthropologist* 71 (August):634-747. Quoted in David Naugle. *Worldview: The history of a concept*, 332-33. Grand Rapids: William B. Eerdmans Publishing Company, 2002.

Orr, James. 1915. Asia Minor. *International standard Bible encyclopedia*. Grand Rapids: Wm. B. Eerdmans.

Packer, J. I. 1990. *A quest for godliness: The Puritan vision of the Christian life*. Wheaton: Crossway Books.

Pink, Arthur W. 1974. *The Ten Commandments*. Swengel, PA: Reiner Publications.

Pliny. *Ep. IV*. Quoted in Jerome Carcopino. *Daily life in ancient Rome: The people and the city at the height of the empire*, 78-9. Ed. Henry T. Rowell, trans. E.O. Lorimer. New Haven: Yale University Press, 1992.

Polanyi, Michael. 1983 (1966). *The tacit dimension*. Gloucester, MD: Peter Smith.

Quintilian. *Institutio Oratoria*. Quoted in Jerome Carcopino. *Daily life in ancient Rome: The people and the city at the height of the empire*, 104. Ed. Henry T. Rowell, trans. E.O. Lorimer. New Haven: Yale University Press, 1992.

Ramsay, William. 1907. *Cities and bishoprics of Phrygia*. Vol. 1. London: Hodder & Stoughton.

_____. 1904. *Letters to the seven churches of Asia and their place in the plan of the Apocalypse*. London: Hodder & Stoughton. http://www.ccel.org/ccel/ramsay/ letters.html [accessed 10/28/2008].

Rashkow, Ilona N. 1990. *Upon the dark places: Anti-antisemitism and sexism in English Renaissance biblical translation*. Bible and Literature Series, no. 28. ed. David M. Gunn. Sheffield: Almond Press.

Redfield, Robert. 1941. *The folk culture of the Yucatan*. Chicago: University of Chicago Press.

Reid, W. Stanford. 1954. The covenant interpretation of culture. *The Evangelical Quarterly* 26, no. 4 (October): 194-209.

Robertson, O. Palmer. 1980. *The Christ of the covenants*. Phillipsburg, NJ: Presbyterian and Reformed Publishing Co.

Rogers, Glenn. 2002. *The role of worldview in missions and multiethnic ministry*. Pasadena, CA: Mission and Ministry Resources.

Rosenberg, Joel. 1984. Biblical narrative. In *Back to the basics: Reading the classic Jewish texts*, ed. Barry W. Holtz. NY: Simon & Schuster Paperbacks.

Rubin, Herbert J., and Irene S. Rubin. 1995. *Qualitative interviewing: The art of hearing data*. Thousand Oaks, CA: Sage Publications. Inc.

Ryken, Leland. 1986. *Worldly saints: The Puritans as they really were*. Grand Rapids: Zondervan.

Schaeffer, Francis A. 1985. *Letters of Francis A. Schaeffer*. Ed. Lane T. Dennis. Wheaton, IL: Crossway Books.

Schmitz, Thomas. 2007. *Modern literary theory and ancient texts*. NJ: John Wiley and Sons.

Seutonius, C. Tranquillus. 1883. *The lives of the twelve Caesars*. Trans. Alexander Thomson. NY: R. Worthington.

Sibley, Laurence C., Jr. 2004. Baptizing the nations: Mission, culture and liturgy in the Gospel of Matthew. Research/writing project for 2003 Luce Seminar, Prospects of Historic Liturgies in a Postmodern Age. Philadelphia: Westminster Theological Seminary.

Simons, H. 1980. *Towards a science of the singular: Essays about case study in educational research and evaluation*. Norwich, UK: University of East Anglia, Centre for Applied Research in Education.

Stackhouse, Max. 1988. *Apologia: Contextualization, globalization, and mission in theological education*. Grand Rapids: William B. Eerdmans Publishing Company.

Stake, R. E. 1995. *The art of case study research*. Thousand Oaks, CA: Sage.

Stamm, J. J. 1967. *The Ten Commandments in recent research*. Trans. M. E. Andrew. *Studies in biblical theology*, vol. 2. Naperville, IL: Alec R. Allenson, Inc.

Strabo. 1903. *Geography*. Trans. H.L. Jones. London: George Bell & Sons. http://www.perseus. tufts.edu/cgi-bin/ ptext?doc=Perseus%3A text %3A1999.01.0239%3Ahead %3D%233 [accessed 01/10/2009].

Tacitus. *Dialogues*. Quoted in Jerome Carcopino. *Daily life in ancient Rome: The people and the city at the height of the empire*, 104. Ed. Henry T. Rowell, trans. E.O. Lorimer. New Haven: Yale University Press, 1992.

Thiselton, Anthony C. 1980. *The two horizons: New Testament hermeneutics and philosophical description*. Grand Rapids: William B. Eerdmans Publishing Company.

_____. 1992. *New Horizons in hermeneutics*. Grand Rapids: Zondervan Publishing House.

Trebilco, Paul. 1994 Asia. In *The Book of Acts in its Graeco-Roman setting*, ed. David W. J. Gill and Conrad Gempf. Grand Rapids: Eerdmans. Quoted in Brandon Wason. *Paul's Ephesus: Ephesus in the Book of Acts*, 2. http://www. novumtestamentum.com/acts/Ephesus/ephesus.html [accessed 12/04/2008].

United Nations of Roma Victrix. Asia Minor. In UNRV history: Roman Empire. http://www.unrv.com/provinces/asia-minor-php [accessed 2/03/2009].

Van Til, Cornelius. 1932. *A survey of Christian epistemology: A syllabus*. Phillipsburg, NJ: The Presbyterian and Reformed Publishing Company.

_____. 1955. *The defense of the faith*. Philadelphia: The Presbyterian and Reformed Publishing Company.

Walcot, Peter. 1973. *Greece and Rome* 20, no. 2 (April):97-100. Cambridge University Press. Quoted in T. P. Wiseman, ed. Competition and co-operation. *Roman political life 90 B.C. to A.D. 69*, 12. Exeter studies in history, no. 7. Ed. Colin James. Exeter University Publication, 1985.

Walls, Andrew F. 2007. *The missionary movement in Christian history: Studies in the transmission of the faith*. Maryknoll, NY: Orbis Books.

Wason, Brandon. 2006. *Paul's Ephesus: Ephesus in the Book of Acts*. http://www.novumtestamentum.com/acts/Ephesus/ ephesus.html [accessed 12/04/2008].

Weinfeld, M. 1973. Covenant terminology in the ancient Near East and its influence on the West. *Journal of the American Oriental Society* 93: 190-273.

T. P. Wiseman, ed. 1985. Competition and co-operation. *Roman political life 90 B.C. to A.D. 69*. Exeter studies in history, no. 7, ed. Colin James. Exeter University Publication.

Wood, Bryant G. 1998. *Israelites in Egypt: Is there evidence?* Christian
    Answers.net. http://www.christiananswers.net/ q-abr/abr-a027.html
    [accessed 10/20/2008].

Wright, Christopher. 1996. Deuteronomy. *New International Biblical
    Commentary*, Old Testament Series. Peabody, MA: Hendrickson
    Publishers.

Wright, N. T. 1996. *The New Testament and the people of God.* Vol 1.
    Minneapolis: Augsburg Fortress.

Yin, Robert K. 1994. *Case study research: Design and methods.* 2d ed. Newbury
    Park, CA: Sage.

Works Consulted

Agar, Michael. 1991. The right brain strikes back. In *Using computers in
    qualitative research*, ed. Nigel G. Fielding and Raymond M. Lee.
    Surrey, UK: Sage Publications, Ltd.

Allen, Charles L. 1965. *The Ten Commandments: An interpretation.* Westwood,
    NJ: Revell.

Aling, Charles F. 1996. The historicity of the Joseph story. Bible and Spade 9: 17-
    28. Quoted in B. G. Wood. *Israelites in Egypt: Is there any evidence?*
    1998. http://www.christiananswers.net/q-abr/abr-a027.html [accessed
    10/20/2008].

Alt, A. 1967. The origins of Israelite law. In *Essays on Old Testament history and
    religion*, trans. R. A. Wilson. New York: Doubleday.

Alter, Robert. 1981. *The art of biblical narrative.* New York: Basic Books.
    Quoted in Ilona N. Rashkow. *Upon the dark places: Anti-antisemitism
    and sexism in English renaissance biblical translation.* Bible and
    Literature Series, ed. David M. Gunn, no. 28, Sheffield: Almond Press,
    1990.

Althaus, Paul. 1972. *The ethics of Martin Luther.* Philadelphia: Fortress.

173

Audet, J., & d'Amboise, G. 2001. The multi-site study: An innovative research methodology. *The Qualitative Report* [On-line serial], 6(2). http://www.nova.edu/ssss/QR/ QR6-2/audet.html [accessed 02/16/2009].

Baieri, Joseph J. 1945. *The commandments explained: According to the psychological method, based on the revised Baltimore catechism and Deharbe's catechism.* St. Paul: Catechetical Guild.

Barclay, William. 1972. *The old law and the new law.* Philadelphia: Westminster Press.

Bisagno, John R. 1979. *Positive obedience: The Christian response to the Ten Commandments.* Grand Rapids: Zondervan.

Black, Harold Garnet. 1945. *Broken pillars: A study of the Ten Commandments.* NY: Fleming H. Revell Co.

Boman, Thorleif. 1970. *Hebrew thought compared with Greek.* NY: W. W. Norton and Company.

Boudouris, Konstantine, and Kostas Kalimtzis, eds. 2008. *Paideia: Education in the global era.* Vol. 2. Athens: Ionia Publications. http://www.hri.org/iagp/books/ vol55.html [accessed 11/25/2008].

Briscoe, D. Stuart. 1986. *Playing by the rules.* Old Tappan, NJ: F. H. Revell.

Brown, William P., ed. 2004. *The Ten Commandments: The reciprocity of faithfulness.* Louisville: Westminster John Knox Press.

Burgess, John P. 2005. *After baptism: Shaping the Christian life.* Louisville, KY: Westminster John Knox Press.

Butterworth, Eric. 1977. *How to break the Ten Commandments.* NY: Harper & Row.

Caldwell, Larry. 1999. Towards the new discipline of ethnohermeneutics: Questioning the relevancy of Western hermeneutical methods in the Asian context. *Journal of Asian Mission* 1, no. 1:21-43.

Calvin, John. 1977. *The Acts of the Apostles: 1-13.* Vol. 6. Calvin's Commentaries. Grand Rapids: Eerdmans.

174

_____. 1958. *Tracts and treatises on the reformation of the church*. Grand Rapids: Eerdmans.

Conn, Harvie M. 1984. *Eternal Word and changing worlds: Theology, anthropology and mission in trialogue*. Grand Rapids: Academie Books.

_____. 1988. Normativity, relevance, and relativism. In *Inerrancy and hermeneutic*, ed. Harvie M. Conn. Grand Rapids: Baker Books.

Cox, William F., Jr., and Nelda S. Haney. 2002. Analysis of Christian character curricula: Development of holy nation citizens. *Journal of research on Christian education* 11, no. 2 (Fall): 121-159.

Crotts, Stephen M. 1987. *Ten Commandments for now*. Fletcher, NC: New Puritan Library.

Dale, R. W. 1899. *The Ten Commandments*. London: Hodder & Stoughton.

Davidman, Joy. 1955. *Smoke on the mountain: The Ten Commandments in terms of today*. London: Hodder & Stoughton.

Day, Gardiner M. 1949. *Old wine in new bottles: A modern interpretation of the Ten Commandments*. NY: Morehouse-Gorham Co.

Denny, Randal E. 1970. *Tables of stone for modern living*. Grand Rapids: Baker Book House.

Dickie, Matthew W. 2003. *Magic and magicians in the Greco-Roman World*. Abingdon, UK: Routledge.

Dillenberger, John, ed. 1961. *Martin Luther: Selections from his writings*. Garden City, NY: Anchor Books.

D'Souza, Keith, and Janina Gomes. 2007. Christian faith: Christian definition of true reality. http://www. experiencefestival.com 02.10.2007.

Dura-Europas. 2008. http://www.sacred-destinations.com/syria/ dura-europos.htm [accessed 03/03/2009].

Dykes, J. Oswald. 1884. *The law of the Ten Words*. London: Hodder & Stoughton.

Edgar, William. 2007. *Les dix commandements*. Charois, France: Editions Excelsis.

Eisenhardt, Kathleen M. 1989. Building theories from case study research. *Academy of management review* 14, no. 4: 532-550.

Farkas, Jovzsef. 1969. *Benchmarks*. Trans. John R. Bodo. Richmond, VA: John Knox Press.

Ferguson, Everett. 1987. *Backgrounds of early Christianity*. Grand Rapids: Eerdmans.

_____. 1999. *Christianity in relation to Jews, Greeks, and Romans.* Recent studies in early Christianity: A collection of scholarly essays. NY: Garland Publishing Company.

_____. 1980. *Greek and Roman religion: A source book*. Park Ridge, NJ: Noyes Press.

Fisher, Wallace E. 1978. *Stand fast in faith: Finding freedom through discipline in the Ten Commandments*. Nashville: Abingdon.

Flowers, H. J. 1927. *The permanent value of the Ten Commandments*. London: G. Allen & Unwin Ltd.

Fluegel, Maurice. 1910. *Exodus, Moses and the decalogue legislation: The central doctrine and regulative organum of Mosaism*. Baltimore, MD: Fluegel Co.

Forell, George W. 1955/70. *Ethics of decision: An introduction to Christian ethics*. Philadelphia: Muhlenberg Press.

Freedman, David N. 2000. *The nine commandments: Uncovering a hidden pattern of crime and punishment in the Hebrew Bible*. Ed. Astrid B. Beck. NY: Doubleday.

Furnish, Victor Paul. 1972. *The love command in the New Testament*. Nashville: Abingdon Press.

Gall, Meredith D., Joyce P. Gall, and Walter R. Borg. 2003. *Educational research: An introduction.* 7th ed. Boston: A. B. Longman.

Gardner, Eugene N. 1958. *Always the Ten Commandments*. Grand Rapids: Eerdmans.

Green, Bryan. 1956. *Being and believing*. London: Hodder & Stoughton.

Samuel Greengus, Samuel. 1992. Law. In *The Anchor Bible Dictionary.* vol. 4. Ed. David Noel Freedman. NY: Bantam Doubleday.

Halsall, Paul, ed. 2001 Internet history sourcebooks: Israel. http://www.fordham.edu/halsall/ancient/ asbook06.html [accessed 11/04/08].

Hanson, Buddy. 2002. *God's Ten Words: A commentary on the Ten Commandments.* Tuscaloosa, AL: Self-published.

Hatch, Edwin. 1957. *The influence of Greek ideas on Christianity.* NY: Harper Torchbooks.

Handelman, Susan A. 1982. *The slayers of Moses: The emergence of rabbinic interpretation in modern literary theory.* Albany: State University of New York Press. Quoted in Ilona N. Rashkow. *Upon the dark places: Anti-antisemitism and sexism in English renaissance biblical translation.* Bible and Literature Series, ed. David M. Gunn, no. 28. Sheffield: Almond Press, 1990.

Hauerwas, Stanley M. and William H. Willimon. 1999. *The truth about God: The Ten Commandments in Christian life.* Nashville: Abingdon Press.

Henry, Carl F. H. 1998. Fortunes of the Christian world view. *Trinity Journal.* http://findarticles.com/p/articles/ mi_qa3803/is_199810/ai_n8814753? tag=untagged [accessed 11/16/2008].

Hiebert, Paul G. 2008. *Transforming worldviews: An anthropological understanding of how people change.* Grand Rapids: Baker Books.

Huesmann, Perry S. 2008. Covenant as ethical commonwealth: Possibilities for trust in an age of Western individualism and disintegration. Master's thesis, Vrije University Amsterdam.

Jacobsen, Thorkild. 1943. Primitive Democracy in Ancient Mesopotamia. *Journal of Near Eastern Studies* 2, no. 172. Quoted in Gerald A. Larue. Old Testament Life and Literature, 1968. http://www.infidels.org/library/ modern/gerald_larue/ [accessed 11/04/2008].

Johnson, Alan F. ed. 1973. *God speaks to an x-rated society: Are the Ten Commandments still valid?* Chicago: Moody Press.

Johnson, Dennis E. 1997. *The message of Acts in the history of redemption*. Phillipsburg, NJ: P&R Publishing.

Kahl, Werner. 2000. Intercultural hermeneutics--contextual exegesis: A model for 21st-century exegesis. *International review of mission* 89, no. 354: 421-433.

Kaiser, Walter C., Jr., and Moisés Silva. 1994. *An introduction to biblical hermeneutics: The search for meaning*. Grand Rapids: Zondervan Publishing House.

Koester, Helmut. 1982. *Introduction to the New Testament*. Vol. 1. NY: Walter de Gruyter.

Koop, Norman A. 1977. *The Ten Commandments*. New Jersey: Word of Truth.

Larkin, William J., Jr. 1988. *Culture and biblical hermeneutics: Interpreting and applying the authoritative Word in a relativistic age*. Eugene, OR: Wipf and Stock, Publishers.

Learning from qualitative data analysis. 2009. http://www. rasch.org/rmt/rmt 91a.htm [accessed 02/11/2009].

Macgreggor, G. H. C., and A. C. Purdy. 1936. *Jew and Greek: Tutors unto Christ. The Jewish and Hellenistic background to the New Testament*. NY: Charles Scribner's Sons.

MacMullen, Ramsey. 1981. *Paganism in the Roman Empire*. New Haven: Yale University Press.

Macmullen, Ramsey, and Eugene N. Lane, eds. 1992. *Paganism and Christianity 100-425 C. E.: A sourcebook*. Minneapolis: Fortress Press.

Martin, Robert K. 1998. Theological education in epistemological perspective: The significance of Michael Polanyi's "personal knowledge" for a theological orientation of theological education. *Teaching theology and religion* 1, no. 3:139-153.

McBain, John M. 1977. *The Ten Commandments in the New Testament*. Nashville: Broadman Press.

McGing, Brian. 2004. Pontus. In *Encyclopedia Iranica*. http:// www.iranica.com/ newsite/index.isc?Article=www.iranica.com/newsite/articles/unicode/ ot_grp5/ot_pontus_20040616.html [accessed 01/10/2009].

Miles, M. B., & A. M. Huberman. 1994. *Qualitative data analysis.* 2d ed. Thousand Oaks, CA: Sage.

Motz, Lotte. 1997. *Faces of the goddess.* Oxford: Oxford University Press.

Mulqueen, Casey, David Baker, and R. Key Dismukes. 2000. Using multifaceted Rasch analysis to examine the effectiveness of Rater training. Paper presented at the 15th Annual Meeting of the Society for Industrial/Organizational Psychology (SIOP) in New Orleans, LA.

Naugle, David. 1992. The Greek concept of *paideia.* Dallas Baptist Seminary paper. http://www.dbu.edu/naugle/pdf/ institute_handouts/paideia/notes.pdf [accessed 03/22/2008].

Neibuhr, Richard. 1956. *Christ and culture.* NY: Harper Perennial.

Newbigin, Lesslie. 1986. *Foolishness to the Greeks.* Grand Rapids: Wm. B. Eerdmans Publishing Company.

Nielsen, Eduard. 1968. *The Ten Commandments in new perspective: A traditio-historical approach.* Trans. David Bourke. London, S. C. M. Press.

Packer, J. I. *The Ten Commandments. I want to be a Christian*, part 4: *Design for life, The Ten Commandments.* Wheaton, IL: Tyndale House Publishing,

Poythress, Vern S. 1999. *God centered biblical interpretation.* Phillipsburg, NJ: P & R Publishing.

Ramsay, William. 1907. *St. Paul the traveler and the Roman citizen.* 10th ed. London: Hodder & Stoughton. http:// www.ccel.org/ccel/ramsay/paul_roman.i.html [accessed 03/10/2009].

_____. 1919. A noble Anatolian family of the fourth century. *The Classical Review*, 33, No. 1/2 (Feb. - Mar.): 1-9.

_____. 2006. "The city and culture of Ephesus." Excerpts. http://www.grovecityalliance.org/2006/PDFsermons/ Ephesians03-Ephesus.pdf [accessed 03/10/2009].

Reed, Gordon. 1983. *Living life by God's law: A study in the Ten Commandments.* Macon, GA: Word Ministries.

Reisinger, Ernest C. 1997. *The law and the gospel.* Phillipsburg, NJ: P&R Publishing Company.

Ricoeur, Paul. 1974. *The conflict of interpretations: Essays in hermeneutics*. Ed. Don Ihde. Evanston, IL: Northwestern University Press.

Sambursky, Samuel. 1987. *The physical world of the Greeks*. Trans. Merton Dagut. Princeton, NJ: Princeton University Press.

Schaeffer, Edith. 1994. *10 things parents must teach their children (and learn for themselves)*. Grand Rapids: Baker Books.

Sire, James. 1997. *The universe next door: A basic worldview catalog.* 3d ed. Downers Grove, IL: InterVarsity Press.

Smaling, A. 2003. Inductive, analogical, and communicative generalization. *International Journal of Qualitative Methods* 2, no. 1. Article 5. http://www.ualberta.ca/ ~iiqm/backissues/2_1/html/smaling.html [accessed 02/16/2009].

Soy, Susan K. 1997. The case study as a research method. Unpublished paper, University of Texas at Austin. http://www.ischool.utexas.edu/~ssoy/usesusers/1391d1b. htm [accessed 11/22/2008].

Stark, David. 1997. The Christian world and life view. http://www.geocities.com/Athens/3150/christianworldand lifeview.html [accessed 08/07/2008].

Steinberg, David. 2003. Impact of Greek culture on normative Judaism. http://www.adath-shalom.ca/greek_influence. htm [accessed 03/03/2009].

Tarnas, Richard. 1991. *The passion of the Western mind*. NY: Ballantine Books.

Tellis, Winston. 1997. Application of a case study methodology. *The qualitative report* 3, n. 3 (September):1-16. http:// www.nova.edu/ssss/QR/QR3-3/tellis2.html [accessed 10/22/2008].

Thiel, B. 2008. Were the Ten Commandments in effect before Mt. Sinai? Cogwriter. http://www.cogwriter.com/ten.htm [accessed 03/03/2009].

Tillich, Paul. 1968. *A complete history of Christian thought*. Ed. Carl E. Braaten. NY: Harper & Row, Publishers.

_____. 1972. *Biblical religion and the search for ultimate reality*. Chicago: University of Chicago Press.

Ulansy, David. 2000. Cultural transition and spiritual transformation: From
        Alexander the Great to cyberspace. In *The vision thing: Myth, politics,
        and psyche in the world*, ed. Thomas Singer. NY: Routledge.

Ulin, Robert. 2007. Revisiting cultural relativism: Old prospects for a new
        cultural critique. *Anthropological quarterly* 80, no. 3 (Summer):803-
        820. http://www.
        neorunner.com/archive/2007/10/04/Revisiting_Cultural_
        Relativism_Old_Prospects_for_a-NewCultural_Critique. php [accessed
        10/12/2007].

Van Hoozer, Kevin J., Charles A. Anderson, and Michael J. Sleasman, eds. 2007.
        Everyday theology: How to read cultural texts and interpret trends.
        Grand Rapids: Baker Academic.

Wood, John. 1877. *Discoveries at Ephesus*. London.

Yenen, Serif. 1997. http://www.turkishodyssey.com/turkey/ history/history.htm
        [accessed 12/08/2008].

181

INDEX OF SUBJECTS

Abraham, Abrahamic 4, 6, 12, 13, 29,
44, 45, 46
Abrahamic covenant 4

assumption, worldview assumption iii,
4, 5, 6, 8, 19, 22, 23, 24, 25, 27, 28,
71, 87, 91, 94, 96, 97, 111, 113,
115, 118, 121, 122, 123, 124, 125

Averbeck, Richard 53, 54, 55, 56, 57,
58, 122

Bavinck, J.H. 12, 25, 26, 115

believer, member of the covenant
community 3, 4, 5, 7, 9, 14, 17,
25, 26, 39, 40, 41, 57, 61, 64, 65,
66, 76, 80, 81, 82, 84, 85, 89, 90,
93, 94, 95, 96, 97, 98, 100, 109,
113, 114, 116, 120, 121, 123, 127,
128, 129, 130, 132, 135

Bellah, Robert 33, 35, 38, 123

biblical, biblically 2, 5, 6, 7, 8, 9, 11,
13, 14, 21, 24, 25, 26, 28, 29, 32,
34, 36, 37, 39, 40, 47, 49, 52, 54,
63, 66, 81, 91, 100, 101, 102, 103,
104, 105, 106, 107, 108, 109, 111,
113, 114, 115, 116, 117, 119, 120,
122, 124, 125, 128
biblical case study 46, 96, 119,
121, 122, 124, 128, 129, 135
biblical covenant, biblical
covenantal theory 3, 7, 8, 11, 17,
18, 24, 25, 26, 56
biblical given 4, 33, 111, 112
biblical hermeneutic 27
biblical ontology 10, 11, 117
non-biblical, unbiblical,
anti-biblical 33, 104, 105, 106,

114, 125
Calvin, Jean 2, 6, 12, 13, 14, 29, 33,
35, 64, 135

Carcopino, Jerome 73, 74, 76, 77, 78,
79, 80, 81

case 30, 31
case law 5, 15, 50, 54, 55, 56, 60,
62, 63, 119, 120
case study iii, 3, 8, 10, 29, 30, 31,
32, 33, 34, 35, 36, 37, 39, 41, 46,
51, 61, 65, 66, 81, 82, 85, 86, 96,
97, 102, 115, 116, 117, 118, 119,
120, 121, 122, 123, 124, 125, 126,
127, 128, 129, 131, 132, 135

Cassuto, Umberto 42, 49, 51, 59

Church, churched 97, 98, 105, 106,
107, 108, 110, 113, 114, 115, 116,
122, 124, 125, 126, 127, 128, 130,
133, 140, 152, 153
unchurched 97, 98, 104, 105, 107,
108, 109, 110, 112, 113, 114, 115,
116, 122, 125, 126, 127, 129, 130,
133, 135
re-churched 133

command, Commandment iii, 3, 5, 6,
7, 9, 35, 40, 53, 55, 56, 57, 60, 61,
66, 85, 87, 96, 97, 99, 101, 105,
109, 110, 115, 127, 128, 132, 133,
135, 144

context 14, 26, 31, 48, 53, 55, 65, 85,
87, 93
contextualization 20

covenant, the Covenant iii, 3, 5, 6, 7,
9, 10, 11, 12, 13, 14, 15, 16, 17, 23,

Daniel V. Porter

Dr. Daniel V. Porter holds a Ph.D. in Intercultural Studies and an M.A. in Theology from the Reformed Theological Seminary in Jackson, Mississippi.